SONG OF SOLOMON

Toni Morrison

AUTHORED by Anna Lis
UPDATED AND REVISED by W.C. Miller

COVER DESIGN by Table XI Partners LLC
COVER PHOTO by Olivia Verma and © 2005 GradeSaver, LLC

BOOK DESIGN by Table XI Partners LLC

Published by GradeSaver LLC, www.gradesaver.com

First published in the United States of America by GradeSaver LLC. 2007

GRADESAVER, the GradeSaver logo and the phrase "Getting you the grade since 1999" are registered trademarks of GradeSaver, LLC

ISBN 978-1-60259-118-9

Printed in the United States of America

For other products and additional information please visit
http://www.gradesaver.com

Table of Contents

Table of Contents

Biography of Toni Morrison (1931-)

Chloe Anthony Wofford, later known as Toni Morrison, was born in Lorain, Ohio, in 1931. She was the daughter of a shipyard welder and a religious woman who sang in the church choir. Her parents had moved to Ohio from the South, hoping to raise their children in an environment more friendly to blacks. Despite the move to the North, the Wofford household was steeped in the oral traditions of Southern African American communities. The songs and stories of Chloe Wofford's childhood undoubtedly influenced her later work; indeed, Toni Morrison's oeuvre draws heavily upon the oral art forms of African Americans. Although Toni Morrison's writing is not autobiographical, she fondly alludes to her past, stating, "I am from the Midwest so I have a special affection for it. My beginnings are always there.... No matter what I write, I begin there.... It's the matrix for me.... Ohio also offers an escape from stereotyped black settings. It is neither plantation nor ghetto."

She was an extremely gifted student, learning to read at an early age and doing well at her studies at an integrated school. Her parents' desire to protect their child from the racist environment of the South succeeded in many respects: racial prejudice was less of a problem in Lorain, Ohio than it would have been in the South, and Chloe Wofford played with a racially diverse group of friends when she was young. Inevitably, however, she began to experience racial discrimination as she and her peers grew older. She graduated with honors in 1949 and went to Howard University in Washington D.C. At Howard, she majored in English and minored in classics, and was actively involved in theater arts through the Howard University Players. She graduated from Howard in 1953 with a B.A. in English and a new name: Toni Wofford (Toni being a shortened version of her middle name). She went on to receive her M.A. in English from Cornell in 1955.

After a teaching stint at Texas Southern University, she returned to Howard University and met Harold Morrison. They married, and before their divorce in 1964 Toni and Harold Morrison had two sons. It was also during this time that she wrote the short story that would become the basis for her first novel, *The Bluest Eye*.

In 1964, she took a job in Syracuse, New York as an associate editor at Random House. She worked as an editor, raised her sons as a single mom, and continued to write fiction. In 1967 she received a promotion to senior editor and a much-desired transfer to New York City. *The Bluest Eye* was published in 1970. The story of a young girl who loses her mind, the novel was well-received by critics but failed commercially. Between 1971 and 1972 Morrison worked as a professor of English for the State University of New York at Purchase while holding her job at Random House and working on *Sula*, a novel about a defiant woman and relations between black females. *Sula* was published in 1973.

The years 1976 and 1977 saw Morrison working as a visiting lecturer at Yale and working on her next novel, *Song of Solomon*. This next novel dealt more fully with black male characters. As with *Sula*, Morrison wrote the novel while holding a teaching position, continuing her work as an editor for Random House, and raising her two sons. *Song of Solomon* was published in 1977 and enjoyed both commercial and critical success. In 1981, Morrison published *Tar Baby*, a novel focusing on a stormy relationship between a man and a woman. In 1983 she left Random House. The next year she took a position at the State University of New York in Albany.

Beloved, the book many consider to be Morrison's masterpiece, was published in 1987. Mythic in scope, *Beloved* tells the story of an emancipated slave woman named Sethe who is haunted by the ghost of the daughter she killed. The novel is an ambitious attempt to grapple with slavery and the tenacity of its legacy. Dedicated to the tens of millions of slaves who died in the trans-Atlantic journey, *Beloved* could be called a foundation story (like Genesis or Exodus) for black America. It became a best seller and received a Pulitzer prize.

In 1987 Toni Morrison became the Robert F. Goheen Professor in the Council of Humanities at Princeton University. She is the first African American female writer to hold a named chair at a university in the Ivy League. She published *Jazz* in 1992, along with a non-fiction book entitled *Playing in the Dark: Whiteness and the Literary Imagination*. The next year she became the eighth woman and the first black woman to receive the Nobel Prize in Literature. 1998 saw the publication of her seventh novel, *Paradise*.

One of the most critically acclaimed living writers, Morrison has been a major architect in creating a literary language for Afro-Americans. Her use of shifting perspective, fragmentary narrative, and a narrative voice extremely close to the consciousness of her characters reveals the influence of writers like Virginia Woolf and William Faulkner: two writers that Morrison, not coincidentally, studied extensively while a college student. All of her work also shows the influence of African-American folklore, songs, and women's gossip. In her attempts to map these oral art forms onto literary modes of representation, Morrison has created a body of work informed by a distinctly black sensibility while drawing a reading audience from across racial boundaries.

About Song of Solomon

Song of Solomon, a rich and empowering novel published in 1977 that focuses on black life across America, follows the path of Milkman Dead, a young black male in search for his identity. Toni Morrison's gift of storytelling clearly shines through her poignant writing, as she presents Dead's search for his culture and history, impeded by the society he lives in. *Song of Solomon* not only focuses on African American community life, it is also a stark depicter of everyday white oppression. The novel earned Toni Morrison a National Book Critics Circle Award and an American Academy and Institute of Arts and Letters Award.

In contrast to her earlier works, *Song of Solomon* encompasses a wide variety of black communities across America, from the liberal Midwest to the old-fashioned and somewhat conservative South. It is a novel that arouses consciousness in the face of an African American struggle of confinement into a life of possibility. *Song of Solomon* is also Morrison's first novel to be written through a male protagonist view, and the narrator's extraordinary manner of weaving in and out creates an even more spellbound lure into the novel's plot. This technique follows in part from the author's interest in folk storytelling traditions; Morrison patterns the novel after a Yoruba folktale about African-born slaves who could fly back to Africa whenever they wanted. Morrison alludes to other ancient storytelling and folk art traditions as well. The title itself comes from the Song of Songs (or Song of Solomon) in the Old Testament, a rhapsodic love poem consisting of addresses between a lover and a beloved. The lyrics of the Song of Solomon as presented in the novel are a variant of a Gullah folktale, further emphasizing the importance of oral tradition. Interestingly, Morrison may have taken this interest in roots and history even further with the name of Solomon, as that was the name of her own grandfather, a former slave.

About Song of Solomon

Character List

Macon Dead III

Known as Milkman Dead, the protagonist of the novel. Born into a prominent and privileged family, Milkman is an egocentric individual who only discovers compassion upon his spiritual rebirth in the deep South. Milkman's discovery of his family history underlines his understanding of flight, not as a means of escape but as a means of living.

Ruth Foster Dead

Milkman's mother and the daughter of Dr. Foster, the first Negro doctor in town. Ruth, emotionally abused by her husband, lives a celibate and loveless existence, focusing all her energy on Milkman. Ruth claims that her father is the only one who cared how she lived. Despite her unhappiness, Ruth stays married to Macon Dead II, a move that exemplifies her passive character and reaffirms her appreciation for the finer life.

Macon Dead II

Milkman's father. A man obsessed with acquiring property, Macon is ruthless in his pursuit of money. His obsession is wedged in his memory of watching his father die trying to protect his land. Macon's unyielding attitude is only softened when he is reminded of stories from his childhood.

First Corinthians Dead

Milkman's sister, referred to as simply Corinthians. Leading a privileged life, she attends Bryn Mawr and travels to France to discover that at forty-three, she has no useful skills and is still unmarried. Corinthians suffers a nervous breakdown, and finds a job as a maid for Michael-Mary Graham. She is intelligent, strives to be independent, and falls in love with Porter, a yardman. Her fervent love affair demonstrates her ability to cross borders, in respect to social class and familial boundaries.

Magdalene Dead

Called Lena, she is another one of Milkman's sisters. Throughout the first half of the book, Lena is characterized by a submissive personality only known for her act of sewing red velvet rose petals. Only her emotional outburst at Milkman's egotistic behavior alludes to her inner strength.

Michael-Mary Graham

The State Poet Laureate. Michael-Mary is charmed by Corinthians name, and hires her on the spot. Although she is a liberal, she does not treat Corinthians as her equal, suggesting a double standard solely based on color.

Henry Porter

A member of the Seven Days society and a yardman, Porter falls in love with Corinthians while seeing her on the bus. Porter's love for Corinthians makes him leave the society, and shows that love can cross over social classes.

Pilate Dead

Macon Dead II's sister. Pilate is a powerful character, both spiritually and emotionally, and is instrumental to the plot of the novel. Born without a nave, Pilate is rejected by society in her younger years but still embraces love to the fullest. She takes care of her daughter and granddaughter altruistically, and is responsible for Milkman's safe birth.

Circe

A midwife who delivers both Macon Dead II and Pilate. Employed by the affluent Butler family, Circe ascertains that their estate is ruined once they have passed away. As her namesake in the Odyssey, she is responsible for leading Milkman "home".

Rebecca

Nicknamed Reba, she is not considered as bright as her mother or daughter. Reba's talent for winning objects emphasizes the idea that one does not need money to succeed. Reba is also renowned for giving men gifts and money, although they do not return her affections.

Sing

Also known as Singing Bird, she is Milkman's great-grandmother. A Native American, Sing's name is the first connection Milkman has to his family history.

Freddie

A janitor who nicknames Macon Dead III as "Milkman". Freddie, the town gossipmonger, is often guilty of misinterpreting his information.

Sweet

A prostitute living in Shalimar, Virginia, whom Milkman has an affair with. She is pretty and easy-going, and it is with her that Milkman reinvents himself as a compassionate and thoughtful man. Their relationship is one of mutual respect.

Solomon

Milkman's great-grandfather, who flies away to Africa to escape his life of slavery. Shortly after beginning his flight, he drops his son Jake. Solomon left behind twenty-one children, and a hysterically-grieving wife. His flight shows the positive and negative effects of escape.

Ryna

Solomon's wife and Milkman's great-grandmother. She is left behind with twenty-one children, and rumor has it that she still wails after her long-lost husband. Ryna's Gulch is named appropriately after her.

Robert Smith

An insurance agent who jumps of No Mercy Hospital in hopes of flying as a means of escape. Robert was a member of the Seven Days society

Guitar Bains

Milkman's best friend and a member of the Seven Days society. His hatred for whites is triggered by his father's death, after which the white factory owner offered his mother a mere forty dollars as compensation. Eventually, Guitar's anger overcomes him and he destroys his and Milkman's friendship.

Hagar

Reba's daughter and Pilate's granddaughter. Hagar begins an affair with Milkman in her twenties and her love for him continues long after he has lost interest in her. Hagar goes mad with grief at Milkman's rejection. She emphasizes the novel's constant theme of rejection and of women who love too hard.

Dr. Foster

Ruth Dead's father and the first Negro doctor in town. Dr. Foster dislikes his own African American heritage. Macon claims Dr. Foster called blacks "cannibals" and that he was a racist. Dr. Foster's triumphant accomplishment of becoming a doctor in his time is a stark contrast to his attitude.

Saul

A local of Shalimar. He strongly dislikes Milkman's city, wealth-inspired ways. Saul, along with another group of men, instigates a fight with Milkman. He and Milkman's differing attitude emphasize the poverty found in the South.

Major Themes

Flight

The concept of flight is clearly addressed in the beginning of the novel with Mr. Smith's jump - his attempt to fly. Although flight may have positive attributes of the possibility of escape, it also contains negative connotations. Escape suggests leaving behind one's old world and thus pain for those left behind. Solomon, who flew back to Africa, leaves behind his wife Ryna and their twenty-one children. Solomon's departure, although happy in the face of his struggle with slavery, is disastrous for Ryna, who goes mad with grief. Milkman's escape from Not Doctor Street, a relief from his daily unhappiness, is devastating for Hagar, who eventually dies from heartbreak. The overall theme of flight, therefore, is associated with abandonment. Although it is an impossible feat, flight is regarded as natural in the novel. It is believed that Milkman's great-grandfather, Solomon, literally flew away by simply spinning around with his arms spread out until he elevated. The community's acceptance of flight as normal highlights Morrison's use of magical realism in her writing. Even the novel's epigraph, "The fathers may soar And the children may know their names," references the theme of flight.

Allusions in Characters' Names

Names hold a special significance in regards to each character. Pilate, a biblical reference to the Roman governor who allowed the execution of Jesus Christ, shares some similar traits with her namesake, such as strength and power. Although she is not cruel in her authority, Pilate is a male name suggesting that she bears the stereotypical characteristics of a man, at least as perceived by society at the time. Circe's name bears homage to the enchantress in Homer's Odyssey, who provides Odysseus with crucial information on how to end his voyage. In *Song of Solomon*, Circe supplies Milkman with segments of his family history, so that he may end his search for his family heritage. Hagar, a biblical name, is a direct explanation of her strained and desperate relationship with Milkman, who abandons her, as can be predicted through the Bible.

The family surname of Dead is a spiritual wordplay. Milkman's family accidentally received the name from white oppressors, thus suggesting that their real name died, and at that point, so did their family history. The importance of names relates to a sense of belonging, to being able to trace one's roots through the ages. Throughout the entire novel, there are continuous references to Milkman being Dead, both in terms of name and character. Upon Milkman's rebirth, he no longer can be called Dead, neither by name nor by personality.

Singing

The theme of singing and songs is a reference not only to the African oral tradition but also to the days of slavery. Slaves, as means of getting through their work on the plantation, sang spirituals. Such songs talked of faith and hope, and how to live with the spirit of God. Singing was a way in which slaves could express their personal feelings, and it was also a means of cheering one another up. Many songs also contained "secret messages," for instance making indirect references to the Underground Railroad.

The act of singing communicates the importance of the oral tradition, demonstrated through Pilate's "Oh Sugarman done fly away..." The song, originally a reference to Solomon, tells the tale of Milkman's great-grandfather. It is this song that transmits Milkman's family history, and steers him towards his spiritual rebirth. Overall, songs underline the rebuilding of a spiritual and emotional bond. In the novel, Pilate, Hagar and Reba all bond through the act of singing. And, after Hagar's death, Reba and Pilate comfort one another through a song.

Racial Injustice

Toni Morrison emphasizes the country's state of racial injustice. Chapter One mentions racial uplift groups and makes note of segregated hospitals to create a focus on race. Further emphasis is placed on white oppression in regards to race as Guitar remembers that his mother received four ten dollar bills for his father's body. The reasons for Guitar's anger towards whites ars reemphasized in his unfair treatment by a white nurse. His hatred grows to transform him into a revengeful fiend who loses his humanity. The Seven Days society, of which Guitar is a member of, takes justice into their own hands.

Abandonment of Women

Throughout the entire novel, women are abandoned by males to fend for themselves. Solomon abandons his wife, Ryna, and Milkman leaves behind Hagar. Whereas Solomon is regarded as a hero for escaping the evils of slavery, Ryna's suffering is regarded as punitive, almost illogical. Although it is she who is left behind with twenty-one children, the town emphasizes Solomon's victory over her misery. Morrison accents the women's hardships to show the double standard society places upon women.

Wealth

The pursuit of money and property is a struggle for which Macon Dead II has sacrificed his humanity. The gold further accents his greed, and his desire for monetary objects consumes Milkman as well. Although Macon's longing to accumulate worldly goods is a sign of bereavement for his father, his manner of mourning soon turns against him. Milkman's search for the gold becomes a search foe his identity, his real inheritance.

The Color White

Throughout the novel, black and white colors are used to differentiate between good and evil. Stereotypically, society associates white with good and black with evil. *Song of Solomon*, on the other hand, presents the color white as a symbol of malevolence. All the white characters as well as white symbols represent wrongdoing and/or violence. Guitar's father's employer, who is white, gives his mother forty dollars for his father's dead body, a suggestion of how much a black man is thought to be worth. Corinthian's employer, white as well, also does not regard her employee as an equal, although she claims her views are liberal. Freddie's description of his mother's death involves a white bull. And the white peacock that Milkman and Guitar chase represents greed.

Glossary of Terms

A.M.E. Zion

African Methodist Episcopal Church. Officially formed in 1821, the church was formed by black Christians who were discriminated against in white places of worship. The church played a great role in the black antislavery movement, and many well known black abolitionists, such as Frederick Douglass, Sojourner Truth, and Harriet Tubman, were members of the church.

Accra

the capital of Ghana.

AKC

American Kennel Club. The largest American organization dealing with purebred dog pedigrees.

Albert Schweitzer

an Alsatian physican, philosopher and theologian who won the Nobel Peace Prize in 1952, partially for founding and funding a hospital in West Africa.

Algonquins

An aboriginal North American tribe who lived on lands stretching from Virginia to the Hudson Bay.

Armistice Day

November 11th, the anniversary of the end of World War I. Today, November 11th is celebrated as Veterans Day as a memory to the veterans of all wars.

B.B.

a reference to B.B. King (Riley B. King), an African-American blues musician.

Bo Diddley

born Ellas Bates, and also referred to as The Originator, he is an influential American rock and roll singer.

Bryn Mawr

A women's liberal arts college, located in Pennsylvania, and founded in 1885.

Committee on Civil Rights

A committee established by President Truman that researched civil rights. It eventually led to the desegregation of the armed forces and the workplace.

Contes de Daudet

French: The Short Stories of Daudet, written by Alphonse Daudet, a french writer who focused on creating real and typical characters.

Corpus Domini Nostri Jesu Christi custodiat animam tuam

"The body of our Lord Jesus Christ, who watches over our souls."

Cutty Sark

a name brand of blended scotch whisky

Earl Grey

an expensive brand of tea

Eleanor Roosevelt

an American political leader and wife of president Franklin Roosevelt. She was an active civil rights advocate.

Emmett Till

An African-American teenager who was murdered by whites in the region of Mississippi. His murderers were acquitted although they later confessed to the crime. His death sparked the Civil Rights Movement.

Erie Lackawanna

A railway formed in 1960 from two mergers whose motto was, "The Friendly Service Route".

Father Divine

An African-American spiritual leader, also called "the Messenger".

Fats

most likely a reference to Antoine Dominique "Fats" Domino, a reknown African-American singer, and a best-selling artist in the 1950s and 1960s.

Four Roses

A brand of bourbon whiskey

Freedmen's Bureau

A federal agency created to help African-Americans during the Reconstruction

Era.

Herbert Hoover

The thirty-first president of the United States. Hoover is often blamed for deepening the Great Depression.

Jack Daniel's

a brand of whisky

Jelly Roll

A nickname for Ferdinand Morton, a famous Jazz composer and pianist.

Katherine Hepburn

a well-known American actress

Lead-belly

a nickname for Huddie William Ledbetter, a renown African-American folk and blues musician.

Lemon

a reference to "Blind" Lemon Jefferson, one of the most influential blues singers of his time.

Lindbergh

Charles Lindbergh, an American aviator, became famous for his non-stop flight from New York to Paris in 1927.

Louise Beavers and Butterfly McQueen

African-American actresses who undertook minor roles, usually those of maids and mammies, in young Hollywood. They set the stage for future black actors.

Malcolm X

A black Muslim Nationalist leader who, as a last resort, supported militant tactics.

Muddy Waters

A nickname for McKinley Morganfield, considered to be one of the best blues singers/musicians of all time.

Neanderthals

An insulting term for primitive and reactionary people.

Orval Faubus

A former Democratic governor of Arkansas who used the National Guard from desegregating Little Rock Central High School.

Pall Mall

a cigarette brand

Prince Charming

a character in many fairy tales, such as Cinderella, Snow White, and Sleeping Beauty. He is typically a prince who comes to the aid of a damsel in distress, and who must somehow liberate her from an evil spell.

Queen Mary

a grand ocean liner, named after the queen of England.

Red Cap

a brand of ale

Sam Sheppard

an American physician convicted of killing his pregnant wife. He served ten years of his sentence until the verdict was overturned in 1966.

Society of Friends

a Christian denomination, commonly referred to as Quakers. They came to the aid of runaway slaves by sneaking them up North. The Quakers have the most members in Africa.

St. Lawrence

a large river that flows from Lake Ontario and drains into the Gulf of St. Lawrence.

Staggerlee

A story, often presented in old folk ballads or blues songs, about a man called Sheldon who shot his friend Lyons. The shooter, Sheldon, has been nicknamed Stagerlee, and is regarded as a villain.

Susquehanna

A long river that flows from upstate New York, through Pennsylvania and Maryland, and ends at Chesapeake Bay.

Tampa Red

born Hudson Woodbridge, Tampa Red was an influential American guitarist. He was also known as The Guitar Wizard.

Waterford Bowl

A city in southeast Ireland reknown for its' crystal. This particular example refers to a crystal Waterford bowl.

Weimaraner

A silver-gray breed of dog, typically used for hunting. Created in Germany, the dog was specifically produced for the noble/aristocratice class.

Wild Turkey

a brand of bourbon whiskey

Short Summary

Mr. Smith, an insurance agent and member of the merciless Seven Days society, attempts to fly away from the No Mercy Hospital roof, and plummets down to his death. In wake of the commotion surrounding his suicide, Ruth Foster becomes the first African-American woman to give birth inside the hospital. Her son, Macon Dead III, the protagonist of the novel, is soon awarded the unflattering nickname of Milkman, so dubbed because Ruth nurses him well past his infancy. In his childhood, Milkman befriends Guitar and becomes acquainted with his aunt Pilate, a relationship Milkman's father forbids. Milkman's father, Macon Dead II, is motivated by money, and he tells his son to, "Own things. And let the things you own own other things. Then you'll own yourself and other people too." Soon, the effects of a prosperous and privileged upbringing leave Milkman naive and egocentric with no spiritual identity.

In his teenage years, Milkman begins a romantic relationship with Hagar, Pilate's granddaughter. Professionally, he assumes the responsibility of acting as his father's helper, which involves fetching the rent money and calculating the account books. In his spare time, Milkman continues to form what appears to be a close-knit friendship with Guitar. Eventually, Guitar confides he is part of the Seven Days society, a group of black males that kill whites as acts of revenge. Although Guitar justifies his actions by proclaiming white people are evil and unnatural, Milkman realizes the depths of Guitar's anger and warns him against losing his humanity. Guitar and Milkman's friendship soon grows strained.

Macon Dead II unexpectedly learns of what Pilate considers her inheritance, hanging in a green sack from the ceiling. Macon beguiles Milkman into burglarizing Pilate's home by offering him half of what is in the sack. Both men believe that Pilate's green bag is filled with gold nuggets which she stole from a cave in her adolescence. Milkman convinces Guitar to be his partner in crime; Guitar is easily persuaded as he needs funds to carry out his deadly Seven Days assignment. To their dismay, the sack contains nothing but human bones, and as a further annoyance, both men are jailed only to be released when Pilate personally comes in to the local police precinct to explain the situation. Milkman's confrontation with the police awakens his comatose character, and he decides to pursue his chase for the gold.

Embarking on a trip to Pennsylvania in order to find the gold, Milkman is bitterly disappointed when the cave he explores is empty. He does, however, come across some of Macon's old acquaintances, such as his midwife Circe and Reverend Cooper, an old friend of Macon Dead I. Circe informs Milkman that his grandfather's real name was Jake, and that his grandmother was an Indian woman by the name of Sing. Now, more so in quest of his family history than the gold, Milkman ventures down to Shalimar, Virginia.

As a newcomer in a small Southern town, Milkman faces some hostility but he quickly learns to feel affection for the intimate rural community setting. Though Milkman doesn't know it, he is being tracked by Guitar, who wants to murder him for supposedly stealing his half of the gold. In Virginia, Milkman discovers his family history, passed on from generation to generation through the form of a song. It is revealed that Milkman's great-grandfather is the legendary Solomon, who flew back to Africa in order to escape the slave plantation life. As a result of his departure, Solomon leaves behind his wife Ryna and their twenty-one children. Solomon's son, Jake, comes to be raised by Heddy, an Indian woman who also has a daughter by the name of Singing Bird. Once grown, Jake and Singing Bird flee North on a wagon full of free slaves.

Milkman's time in Virginia is a spiritual awakening, and he returns north as a newly compassionate and altruistic human being. News at the home front is dismal, as Hagar has died of a broken heart on his account. To counterbalance Hagar's tragic death, Milkman informs Pilate that the bones she has been carrying in her sack are those of Jake, her father. Milkman and Pilate then travel to Shalimar, Virginia to bury Jake's remains when a bullet intended for Milkman accidentally kills Pilate. Devastated at his recent loss but spiritually reborn, Milkman leaps towards Guitar, knowing that if "you surrendered to the air, you could ride it."

Summary and Analysis of Chapter 1

Summary

On a snowy February afternoon, a North Carolina Mutual Life Insurance agent by the name of Robert Smith jumps to his death from the rooftop of No Mercy Hospital to the pavement of Not Doctor Street. Although Mr. Smith posts a note two days in advance informing everyone of his plans to "fly away," only those who happened to be there witness the suicide. Not Doctor Street, previously called Doctor Street and originally known as Mains Avenue, was a tribute to the only colored doctor the city ever had. In the doctor's living days, the street was known as Doctor Street, and upon his death it became called Not Doctor Street. No Mercy Hospital, so termed because of its' refusal to admit blacks, actually admitted a Negro expectant mother on the day of Mr. Smith's fateful flight.

Ruth Dead, the dead doctor's daughter and the first colored woman to be admitted into No Mercy Hospital, happens to be walking by the hospital with her two teenage daughters on her way to deliver red velvet roses to Gerhardt's Department Store. Upon seeing Robert Smith jump, with blue silk wings flailing about him, Ruth experiences labor pains while her daughters, Magdalena Dead and First Corinthians Dead, drop their basket of red velvet roses. To add to the commotion, a poorly dressed woman named Pilate begins to sing, "O Sugarman done fly away, Sugarman done gone..." The day after Mr. Smith's jump, Ruth Dead gives birth to a son who is named Macon Dead III, after his father.

Ruth, along with her husband and three children, lives in an old, twelve-room house. She is hated and abused by her husband, Macon Dead II, a tyrannical man who inspires fear in all of the house's inhabitants. As the result of sexual deprivation in her marriage, Ruth engages in daily little pleasures, one being the act of rubbing down a water mark on her mahogany table, the other of nursing her son until he was four and too old for it. One day, as she sits in the dead Doctor's study, nursing her son, a flunky and tenant named Freddie glimpses them through a window. His look of surprise confirms that the act of nursing her son at that age may be wrong and strange. And, although she tries to quickly regain her composure, Freddie runs to town and informs everyone of what he saw. Thus, Macon Dead III comes to be given the nickname "Milkman," and it sticks for life.

At the age of four, Milkman discovers that only planes and birds are able to physically fly. This particular discovery depresses him so much so that he even loses his imagination. He soon becomes dull and peculiar. His father does not bestow any attention on him, except when to offer a negative reprimand. Milkman's father, Macon, never approves of his son's nickname and associates it with something dirty and hot. However no one dares tell him the circumstances behind the nickname. Macon Dead II's only concern being money, he is quick to reject anyone's excuses for not being able to pay rent, including Guitar Bain's grandmother, who as a result will end up in the street with a band of grandchildren. Macon also shows no remorse for a tenant by the name of Porter, who one day gets drunk, and while hanging out his attic window with a shotgun in his hand, screams obscenities out to the crowds. Instead of helping the man, Macon's one concern is to get the drunk man's money before he spends it all on alcohol.

During the day, Macon reflects on his family history, particularly thinking of names. Macon was given his name by his father, who in turn received his name from a drunken Yankee in the Union Army. The women in his family, however, followed an old tradition of blindly selecting a name at random out of the bible. And so, Macon's sister, came to be named "Pilate" while his two daughters were called Magdalena and First Corinthians, respectively Lena and Corinthians. Pilate, whom Macon was disgusted by and ashamed of, lived in a slum with her daughter, Rebecca, and granddaughter. Neither Pilate nor Rebecca, called Reba, had husbands and all women were content to live in a slum as bootleggers, and sing in the street for change.

One day, tired after his experience with the drunken Mr. Porter, Macon decides to take a shortcut home that will take him past Pilate's dark single-story house on Darling Street. As he studies Pilate's home, Macon recalls how his own mother died after giving birth to her. In his mind, Macon recounts the story of her birth, which people claimed was abnormal, since she never had a belly button. Inching closer to the electricity-deprived home, Macon hears singing, and looks through the window to find Pilate stirring what was possibly wine, Hagar braiding her hair, and Reba cutting her toenails. Even as their singing voices come to a slow halt, Macon Dead finds himself emotionally mesmerized by the candlelit sight of the three women.

Analysis

Chapter One begins with Mr. Smith's flight, or in other words, death. The themes of both death and flight represent the possibility of escape. Unfortunately, as Mr. Smith plummets to his death, his blue wings failing to carry him, he is only able to escape his life through death. His flight, therefore, was unsuccessful. As a young child, Macon also discovers that he cannot fly. His realization of being suffocated by his mother's needs and wants, and by feeling the oppression his father forces onto his family, Milkman feels trapped with no possibility of escape. The ongoing idea of flight also relates to the overall theme of freedom in African American tradition and literature. The concept of being free, a legally free man or woman, or searching for a way to acquire that freedom is oftentimes expressed through flight.

The fact that Mr. Smith's flight had a negative outcome reflects on the current situation of the novel's characters. Ruth is practically confined to her dark and lonely home, and as she is submissively stuck in a loveless marriage. Macon Dead III, although he is the most powerful black man in his town, is actually trapped by his wealth. His pursuit of money controls his thoughts and feelings, leaving him emotionally unresponsive to nearly everyone. He only becomes positively emotionally aroused when he spies on his sister and her family. Ironically, he has to observe them in hiding. Many of the other characters, such as Porter or Mrs. Bains, are trapped by poverty and unfortunately show no motivation to try to escape their confines.

The emphasis on names represents Macon's lack of identity. He himself feels disconnected with his past, as he cannot himself trace his ancestry. Macon himself remarks upon the fact that there has to be at least one person in his family with a real name, a name "given to him at birth with love and seriousness." Then, he realizes that even if such a person existed, he would never be able to find him or her. Also, just as names are meaningful as part of the story plot, they also carry with them a hidden meaning many times in reference to the bible. For example, Ruth's biblical counterpart, Ruth the Moabite, seeks acceptance from the Hebrews after being estranged by her native peoples. Ruth Foster Dead has also been rejected by the black community for her finer mannerisms but is not accepted in the white community because of her skin color. Interestingly, Ruth has a light yellow skin tone in contrast to her son, Milkman, who is very dark.

The act of the black townspeople renaming the streets signifies an attempt to create their own identity within a community. As the first black woman to give birth in Mercy Hospital, specifically called No Mercy by the black population, Ruth crosses an important racial barrier. Race and racism plays an important theme in the entire novel. Already on the second page we find a white woman carelessly addressing a black woman, ignoring a young boy's correction of her own spelling mistake. Guitar Bains' future hatred and mistrust for whites and Milkman himself may be rooted in his experience with the ignorant white nurse and with the painstakingly cold manner in which Macon evicted him and his grandmother.

Over the centuries, themes of flight and escape have been prevalent in many societies. We have the Greek myth of Icarus whose fax wings failed to carry him, causing his death. We have the children's tale of Peter Pan whose storyline revolves around a young boy escaping to Neverland. Similarly, *Song of Solomon* is based on an African American folktale about slaves being able to fly back to Africa whenever they want to.

Summary and Analysis of Chapter 2

Summary

Every Sunday, the Deads pile into Macon's plush green Packard for a ride about town, mostly to convince Macon himself that he was indeed a successful man. One particular Sunday, as the family was driving up to Honore Lake because Macon was debating on investing in beach houses, Milkman decided that he could no longer wait to use the bathroom. As the car halted to a stop on the side of the street, Lena accompanied Milkman into the woods so that he could relieve himself. While he was doing so, Lena wandered around picking flowers and then headed back by Milkman. Hearing her approaching footsteps, Milkman turned around while still in the act of urinating, and wet Lena's dress. Milkman's habit of constantly turning around and looking back indicates to him that there was no future to look forward to.

However, although there may have been no future in sight, life progressed and at the age of twelve, Milkman had befriended Guitar, a mature high-schooler, and met his aunt Pilate. Their relationship began one day when the two boys purposely came across Pilate, dressed in all black, sitting on the front steps of her home peeling an orange. After a preliminary introduction in which Milkman screamingly defends his name when Pilate says there are only three Deads alive, the boys are eager to get inside Pilate's wine house. Accepting Pilate's offer of soft-boiled eggs, they follow the tall, skinny, unkempt woman into a large sunny space where the odor of fermenting fruit permeates the air.

With the wine smell making both boys drowsy, Pilate is free to talk continuously about her childhood experiences. Pilate talks about the gratitude she feels for Macon for saving her life twice, once during her birth and once again in the dark woods. She talks about her father being blown five feet into the air while sitting on a fence on his own farm in Montour County, Pennsylvania. And, after her father's death, she claims that she and Macon saw his ghost sitting atop a stump in the forest, an experience that left that them shaking like leaves.

As Pilate talks on, the mellow scene is interrupted when Reba and Hagar arrive home, struggling with five-bushel baskets of what looked like brambles. Milkman instantly falls in love with Hagar, prior to even seeing her face. He is introduced to Hagar as her brother, as Pilate states one should act the same towards cousins as towards brothers. As the night progresses, the women tell stories while mashing berries for the wine. They laugh about Reba's luck of winning a diamond ring at Sears' for being the 500,000th customer, when she only walked into the store to use a washroom. In fact, Reba's luckiness is a source of pride to her, having won everything from one hundred pounds of free groceries to diamonds, she claims now no one will sell her a raffle ticket lest she win. The easy-going conversation turns morose as Hagar says she has been hungry, but not in respects to food. The night ends with Pilate, Reba and Hagar singing away in perfect harmony, "Oh Sugarman done fly away..."

Milkman's practically perfect day ended when he arrived home to find his father waiting for him. Freddie had told Macon about Milkman's whereabouts and the two engage in a verbal argument resulting from an emotional power struggle. Milkman ends the argument by beginning a discussion with Macon on how he felt about his father when he himself was twelve. With that, Macon tells the tale of his childhood days of working alongside his father, and the farm he lived on, which boasted a fortune in trees, a stream full of fish, a big barn with a four-stall hog pen, and a four acre pond. He reminisces about a cherry pie Pilate tried to make for him from the farm's own fruit trees. Macon also elaborates on how his father lost his farm, blaming the man's illiteracy for every negative thing that happened to him in his life. It turns out that Macon Dead I had signed a piece of paper which officially signed his property over to a white family. And, as Pilate previously recalls, he died sitting on his fence trying to keep possession of his property. Also, the reason for the clerical mistake behind the accidental Dead family name switch occurred because his father could not read to correct the wrongly entered information. When Milkman inquires about his grandfather's first name, Macon instead comments on how his mother was light-skinned and pretty.

The father and son conversation draws to a close when Macon once again reaffirms his negative feelings about Pilate. Macon claims she does not look normal and that she is a snake ready to cut throats. As his father tells him he is banned from associating with Pilate, Milkman asks questions in hopes of understanding why his father claims that she is a snake. Macon's response indicates that although he thinks Pilate can teach Milkman something in the next life, she is useless in this one. As for Milkman's own productivity, Macon informs him that starting Monday Milkman will be learning the real estate business.

Analysis

Even as a young boy, Milkman wariness towards the future is reflected in his actions. The narrator informs us that he is constantly turning around in order to see what is behind him. Such behavior indicates that he is aware, if only subconsciously, of the lack of future in front of him. Such behavior also emphasizes the importance of having a past, and generally relates to the concept of identity.

As previously mentioned, Macon Dead II has an unsettling desire to accumulate wealth. This love for material possessions was instigated through watching his father die trying to defend his property. As a result, Macon Dead II has rejected natural loves of humanity, instead preferring wealth and power to a happy, spiritual existence. Milkman has inherited his father's lack of spirituality, and appears to be heading down the same path of destruction. And yet, some glimmerings of hope are visible because even as a child Milkman inquires about his family history, specifically about his grandfather's name. Milkman's interest in his identity suggests that he may choose a different path from his father after all.

While many of the characters are emotionally, and perhaps physically, trapped within their own circumstances, Pilate appears to be the only one is liberated. She carries a secret knowledge within her, suggesting she is in control of her destiny and identity. Ironically, just as Macon is well-dressed with a contaminated character, Pilate is unkempt from the outside but clean and pure on the inside. She rejects any desire for material possessions, and is sure of her ground in this world. It is Pilate who, in the last chapter, inspires emotion in the typically cold Macon Dead II. She also inspires a quest of identity in Milkman, who only after visiting her begins inquiring about his family's past.

Both Pilate and Macon Dead II discuss growing up on their father's farm, yet their accounts somewhat differ due to omission. Milkman's father does not recount his experience in coming across his father's ghost while Pilate stresses this event. She claims that it scared her, and her openness in discussing the event shows that she is aware of the fact that she is still haunted, emotionally and spiritually, by her father's death. In admitting that she is haunted, Pilate understands that there is a family problem extending from generation to generation. Macon Dead II's omission of the accident may be interpreted on different levels. Perhaps he purposely did not discuss the accident or else he may have simply forgotten. In either sense, he clearly does not want to be reminded of the spiritual problem he is facing, or he may be completely unaware of it.

Summary and Analysis of Chapter 3

Summary

Milkman now has more time to spend with Pilate, Hagar and Guitar, as he is constantly sent off to pick up rent money in the Southside. Although Guitar is oftentimes busy, Milkman occasionally ditches school in order to be with his friend. On one such day, Guitar takes Milkman to Feather's Pool Hall on Tenth Street, located in the middle of the Blood Bank area, so termed because blood flowed very easily in that particular section of the Southside. Inside, Guitar asks Feather to serve them two beers, but is refused on account of Milkman, because he is Macon Dead's son. Guitar, unable to convince Feather that they can stay, leaves with Milkman, and the two boys wander around town until they arrive at a barbershop, owned by Railroad Tommy and Hospital Tommy.

At fourteen, Milkman begins to believe that one of his legs is shorter than the other. He works at masking this defect, always crossing his left ankle over the right or dancing stiff-legged so that it would not be noticeable to others. Although this defect was partly in his imagination, it served as a basis for his belief that he would never be able to emulate his father. As he could not grow to be like Macon, Milkman chooses to be the opposite of his father, both in character and in appearance. However, Milkman continues to be a good employee to his father, always doing his best and always fetching the rent money from the tenants. And Macon is delighted in his son, partly for his work ethic but mostly for he now had the time to pore over bank papers to decide which plots of land were worth investing in. Of foremost importance to Macon is his belief that his son now belonged to him and not to Ruth.

One day, at what started out as pleasant dinner conversation, Ruth describes her experience of attending her father's former patient Mrs. Djvorak's daughter's Catholic wedding ceremony. Ruth herself being a Methodist, she discloses the fact that she had no idea that only Catholics were allowed to receive communion. Ruth's pretense of innocence drives Macon into a rage; he accuses Ruth of being "silly woman" who by herself "ain't nobody." Ruth's following admission of her being her "daddy's daughter" only proceeds to provoke Macon even further, and he smashes her jaw with his fist right there at the dinner table. Milkman, witness to the aforementioned events, grabs his father by his shirt collar and lets him aggressively know that if Macon touches Ruth one more time, Milkman will kill him.

Shortly after their physical altercation, Macon visits Milkman's room to offer an explanation of his actions to Ruth. Although Milkman resists hearing the information, Macon proceeds to disclose that the Doctor delivered both Lena and Corinthians, explicitly against Macon's wishes. A father delivering his daughter's children was sexually inappropriate in Macon's eyes, and he had wanted a midwife to deliver his children. Macon then recounts the events leading up to and after the Doctor's death, ending with the story of finding Ruth naked, cuddled up in a bed with the dead Doctor, sucking on his white, bloated fingers. Disturbed, Macon wonders if perhaps Ruth had a sexual relationship with her father, and not being able to shake that image, he begins finding Ruth sexually repulsive.

After this disturbing encounter, Milkman searches for Guitar and finds him at Tommy's Barbershop, where everyone is listening to the radio. The radio announcer releases information about a recently murdered black man named Till, who was killed by whites because he had whistled at a white woman and spoke freely of sleeping with them. All present and listening are appalled and angry. Freddie thinks Till should not have acted like a big man from up North. Porter angrily claims that even if they catch the perpetrators, no white man will be sentenced for killing a black man. Guitar, fuming, states that no one should die for whistling at a white lady.

Guitar and Milkman walk to Mary's bar/lounge and order two Scotches. Milkman delves into his fight and conversation with his father, deeply distressed over the physical altercation. Milkman wonders why blacks can't receive their names "the right way." Milkman even ponders what Hagar's last name might be, then he states that his own grandfather received his name from a white man. Upset over how his family name came to be, Milkman says someone should have shot his grandfather, to which Guitar responds, "What for? He was already Dead."

Analysis

Chapter Three shows Milkman growing into a man dominated by egocentric beliefs. Milkman's act of standing up to his father is a means for Milkman to prove his manhood to himself. Acknowledging that he does not have strong feelings of love for his mother, he nevertheless feels glee when he defends her. After his father's talk, Milkman's self-centered attitude comes into view again. Milkman is not unsympathetic to his father's views but he does not have the ability to relate to him. Afterwards, while looking for Guitar, Milkman decides that his family is crazy.

Ruth establishes her inner resilience at the dinner table. As a woman who has been married to her husband for over thirty-five years, Ruth knows how Macon will react when she states that she is her father's daughter. Her private knowledge in this matter gives her the strength she needs to continue living a loveless life. Also, her words are a tribute to her father, Dr. Foster, whom she loved and admired.

Upon reflecting to himself, Milkman also acknowledges the fact that he never thought of Ruth as having a role in life outside of being his mother. Once again, such an attitude reflects his belief that the world revolves around him. Milkman also thinks that he is a ladies' man, and is content with his looks, describing his teeth as "splendid" and his jaw as "firm." Milkman's only insecurity dwells in his belief that his one leg is shorter than the other. This not only distinguishes him from his father, but from the rest of humanity. Milkman's limp and his wealthy upbringing are handicaps that he must surpass in order to escape his sheltered outlook on life.

As Milkman walks down the street, emphasis is placed on traffic walking against him and Milkman being the only one walking in the other direction. Here, one can see that Milkman is different than other people, both in terms of thought and behavior. His uniqueness is once again articulated when he does not cross over to the other side of the street. However, his ability to keep going suggests that he may be brave and strong enough to win whatever challenges or battles he faces. Milkman's overall realization that he is somehow alienated from society begins his quest to develop a more conscientious mind-set.

Milkman irrelevant approach to Guitar's viewpoint is not only a sign of Milkman's ignorance but suggests a broadening gulf between the two friends. Milkman disregards what Guitar speaks of mostly because he cannot relate to it and therefore dismisses it as immaterial. Guitar's speech, a reflection of his poverty-stricken background, relates what he sees around him to oppression and racism. Milkman, immune to such oppression because of a luxurious lifestyle, lives his life in boredom and does not understand Guitar's hostility. Their conversation foreshadows future tension between the two friends.

Summary and Analysis of Chapter 4

Summary

Milkman once again does his Christmas shopping at a Rexell drugstore, selecting a compact for Corinthians, dusting powder and cologne for Lena, chocolates for his mother, and some shaving tools for his father. Milkman is only puzzled as to what he should buy for Hagar, having decided that he no longer wants to keep up the business of seeing her. She still deserves a gift, and Milkman soon comes to the decision to instead give her a nice lump sum of money, along with a carefully written letter explaining his reluctance to see her because they are cousins. Milkman signs the letter with love and gratitude, and a thank you, which sends Hagar into a frenzied state of mind in which she at times loses control over her actions and emotions.

Milkman then sits for a while at his father's desk going over the account books. He is distracted and on edge, only partially because of Hagar, and he recalls a conversation he had with Guitar. Some time ago, a white boy of about sixteen, had been found strangled with his head bashed in. Rumors as to who committed the murder were floating around, and although some joked that it was Winnie Ruth, a white asylum escapee, there was an unspoken feeling of dread and terror in the Southside. The police said that a witness saw a bushy-haired Negro escaping the scene of the schoolyard, where the crime was committed. As Milkman and Guitar walked down Tenth Street, Milkman suggested that some men in Tommy's were aware of too many details surrounding the killing, and that maybe one of them did it. Guitar says that he and Milkman are too different to talk about the same things. Upset, Milkman informs Guitar that they aren't living in Montgomery, Alabama, and he needn't be angry at every Negro who isn't scrubbing floors or picking cotton. Guitar then asks Milkman hypothetically, what if they were living in Montgomery, to which Milkman replies that he would buy a plane ticket.

Milkman describes a dream to Guitar; he is standing at his kitchen sink, looking out the window, and seeing Ruth planting bulbs in the garden. These bulbs sprout tulips that seem to smother her, leaving her kicking against the entangled mass of flowers. Guitar listens to the story, and then asks Milkman why he didn't help her, but Milkman responds that she liked it. Their conversation ends on a sour note as Guitar tells Milkman that it looks like everyone is going down the wrong side of the street but him.

Milkman recalls the aforementioned conversation, and decides that he is unable to finish calculating the account books. He thinks about his life, deciding that he has few meaningful interests, and realizes that he finds money, politics, and racial problems boring. Still debating on how to tackle his future, Freddie stops by the office, badly in need of something hot to drink. Freddie sits down, eager to relax, because he has been running around delivering packages for the department store he works at. Both men are sitting at the desk, indulging in idle chatter, when Freddie makes a comment about being an orphan. Intrigued, Milkman pushes the man to divulge what happened to him in childhood. Freddie responds that on account of how his mother died, no one had wanted to take him in, and he had to be raised in jail as there were no orphanages for colored babies back then.

Freddie then tells Milkman he believes in ghosts, and that his mother was actually killed by a ghost. Freddie claims that as his mother was in the final stages of pregnancy, she was walking down the street with a neighbor when they saw a woman coming down the road. As soon as the neighbor greeted this woman, the woman became a white bull. As a result, Freddie mother fell to the floor and gave birth to him right then and there. When he was delivered, and his mother saw him, she screamed and passed out to never regain consciousness. And so, no one had wanted to take Freddie into their home as a child, because he came into this world brought by a white bull. Freddie's tale of his birth makes Milkman laugh hilariously, however, instead of looking hurt, Freddie only looks surprised.

He and Milkman begin a new topic and Freddie suggests that Guitar has been hiding Empire State, a mute Negro who may be accused of strangling the white boy. Not wanting to believe Freddie, Milkman assures himself Freddie is only trying to get back at him for laughing at his white bull story. Freddie seems quite genial, though, and after wishing Milkman and his parents a Merry Christmas and a New Year, he tells Milkman that Corinthians also knows about the strange things that have been occurring.

Analysis

In Chapter Four, magical realism is entwined into historical settings of the novel. Magical realism is a literary form in which magical elements appear in a setting that is otherwise realistic. Freddie's description of the white bull that killed his mother is an example of using magical realism to denote racial oppression, specifically the domination of whites over blacks. Milkman's vision of seeing Ruth overtaken by tulips is another example of magical realism, in which Ruth's submission is clear as she welcomes the terrorizing tulips that will eventually strangle her.

Milkman's rejection of Hagar's love is an example of his self-centered and callous behavior. Unable to relate to others, Milkman is unable to put himself in Hagar's shoes. Moreover, he does not realize that the impersonal tone he undertakes in the letter is what drove Hagar mad. Hagar, as the other characters in the novel, relates to her biblical namesake. In the Bible, Abraham banishes his concubine Hagar after she bears him a child. Milkman also abandons his lover Hagar once he no longer has any use for her body.

Once again, Milkman and Guitar undergo an unfriendly verbal discussion in which Guitar states that he and Milkman are different. Guitar's continuing emphasis on their differences begins an emotional and physical separation of their friendship. Milkman is reminded of his individuality in a town where everyone appears to be very similar. This is reflected in his reminiscing about the time he was walking against pedestrian traffic. Guitar's then states that he knows where he is going, as if to underline the fact that Milkman is lost both spiritually and emotionally.

Milkman is the only character in the novel reluctant to believe in supernatural events. He tends to refer to such events as dreams, as he does when he is telling Guitar about the killer tulips. Milkman also thinks that his struggle against the people-filled street was also a dream, a dream in which Guitar was walking against him. Milkman's lack of desire to believe in anything but the physical world is a sign that he is lacking in the emotional and spiritual worlds. It is also signifies that he is unable to create bonds with anything other than the physical.

Summary and Analysis of Chapter 5

Summary

While Milkman and Guitar's quarrel over Alabama and Honore creates some distance between the two friends, it also serves as a cleansing for the both of them. And so, when Milkman arrives on Guitar's doorstep to spend the night at his home, he is warmly received and invited for some tea or coffee, since Guitar no longer drinks alcohol. As he is preparing the tea, Guitar rambles on about oppressed peoples and geographical differences between the Northerners and the Southerners.

Hagar, possessed by her maddening love for Milkman, has taken to prowling at night in hopes of catching him helpless enough to kill him. Thus, Milkman spends the night by Guitars' house, half hoping she will kill him. As he lies in bed that night, Milkman recalls how one week earlier he had spotted and followed his mother sneaking out of the house at night to board a bus and then a train, only to arrive at Fairfield Cemetery, where Dr. Foster was buried. As his mother enters the cemetery, Milkman waits at the entrance and confronts her about her relationship with her father.

Silent for forty-five minutes while waiting for the train, Ruth finally states that she loved her father because he was the only one that cared whether she lived and how she lived. Ruth also tells Milkman that Macon killed her father by throwing away all his medication, and that he tried to kill Milkman while he was still in the womb but did not succeed thanks to Pilate. Ruth explains that she and Macon did not have any sexual relations after the birth of Lena and Corinthians until Pilate moved to town. Pilate took control of the situation, created an aphrodisiac that Ruth put in Macon's food, and Milkman was conceived. Milkman then demands to know the truth, if she truly was in bed with her father when he was dead, and also, if she nursed him until he was too old and why. Ruth acknowledges that she laid down next to the doctor in her slip, only to kiss his beautiful fingers good-by, and she claims that while she did in fact breast-feed Milkman past infancy she also prayed for him on her knees.

Milkman continues to lie in Guitar's bed as he hears Hagar break the window in attempts to enter the room. It takes her a long time to raise the window and climb in, but Milkman refuses to even move let alone look at her. In his mind, he wishes her dead but she slowly comes at him and lowers the big butcher knife she is carrying. The knife bounces off Milkman's shoulder blade into his neck, but it is a poorly angled, weak blow. Milkman gets up, looks her in the eyes and after making some cruel remarks to her, leaves.

Ruth finally finds out that Hagar has been trying to kill Milkman as often once a month for the past six moths, and she is livid with fury at the woman who is trying to take away her single passion left in this world. Determined, Ruth boards a bus to visit Pilate, and in the meantime reflects on the last time she went to visit Pilate, over thirty years before. Ruth had lastly seen Pilate when she had come by her house for help on controlling Macon's rages against her pregnancy. Macon, long unaffected by the aphrodisiac, was furious at Ruth for becoming pregnant and was trying to force her to have an abortion. Scared for the life of her unborn child, Ruth reached out to Pilate, who created a voodoo doll of Macon and placed it in his office.

On Pilate's porch, Ruth threatens Hagar and the two begin discussing their love for Milkman. Pilate overhears the two women bickering and tells them that Macon is his own person and whatever he needs, neither one of them have it. Afterwards, Pilate invites Ruth inside and offers her some peaches, and tells Ruth her story of being born without a navel and the negativity she had encountered because of it.

Pilate's tale ends with her deciding to move her daughter, Reba, and her granddaughter, Hagar to her brother's town. Unfortunately, after this relocation, Pilate finds Macon to be inhospitable and unforgiving but she does not move on for Ruth's sake.

Analysis

There is an overall theme of males abandoning women prevalent throughout the novel, and it is emphasized in Chapter Five. Hagar's reaction to Milkman's abandonment discloses her vulnerable nature, and her need for a male presence in her life. Hagar's love for Milkman is overwhelming; as a woman who cannot control her actions, Hagar ultimately becomes dominated by Milkman even after he leaves her. Hagar's submissiveness into her role reflects the male dominated society of that time. Hagar relies on Milkman for her emotional survival, and in fact, she cannot live without him. Her reliance on a man may be interpreted on two levels. Firstly, it is a reference to the overall theme of the novel that many women love too deeply and too strongly, and are then left behind with only their sorrow. Secondly, Hagar's male-based survival may be a reminder for women to support themselves financially without a male. Ruth, as another example, is dependent on Macon Dead II financially and will not leave her loveless marriage so as not to lower her social status.

Ruth and Hagar, although very different on most accounts, share the problem of loving Milkman. They are both consumed with love for him, and need him for their own secret reasons. For Ruth, Milkman marks her winning fight with Macon over their love life. For Hagar, Milkman is the sole emotional support of her existence. Both women think they need Milkman for their survival, and Hagar eventually does. As long as the women remain selfish in their want of acquiring Milkman, they will both remain oppressed.

Pilate, on the other hand, does not rely on men either financially or emotionally, and as a result, she is the novel's strongest female character, in terms of spiritual and emotional endurance. Pilate, unlike other female characters, is strong and powerful. She supports herself financially by making wine. She is suspected to have supernatural powers as a result of her non-existent navel. Pilate is named after Pontius Pilate, the Roman leader who ordered Jesus' crucifixion, and who was an evil and powerful man. Although not evil, Pilate certainly embodies some very positive attributes of power. Ironically, as the only strong and independent character in the novel, Pilate has a male name.

Toni Morrison engages a socio-historical debate in her writing of *Song of Solomon*. Presenting two social groups on different ends of the spectrum, she shows the readers the differences in typical African American ideology. The differences of attitude between Milkman and Guitar represent the two most common black ideologies in terms of achieving true freedom. Milkman, laid back in attitude, is a stark contrast to Guitar, whose hostility commands the use of physical force. Milkman himself compares Guitar to Malcolm X, even to the point of suggesting that Guitar adopt a similar sounding name. Malcolm X, who encouraged force when necessary, wanted to combat what he regarded as white "oppression." Guitar's character embodies Malcolm X's beliefs to the fullest, even taking them to an extreme level as a member of the Seven Days society.

Summary and Analysis of Chapters 6 & 7

Summary

Guitar finally discloses the reasons behind his secretiveness and political interests. He is part of a society called the Seven Days, who kill white people for every time black people are killed and their white killers go unpunished. Composed of seven men, each man is responsible for one day of the week. The Seven Days society tries to make each revenge killing resemble the original. For example, if a black woman is raped and murdered, the Seven Days will at random choose a white woman to rape and murder. Each revenge killing takes place on the same day that the original killing took place. Guitar is the youngest of all the men in the society.

Guitar explains his reasoning to Milkman, stating that he is only trying to keep the ratio of blacks and whites equal, and that whites are unnatural because they enjoy killing for fun. Stating it is in white people's chromosomes to murder, Guitar says no white man is immune from the blood running through his veins. Guitar claims that Hitler only killed the Jews because there were no blacks around. It is therefore necessary for the black people to avenge themselves since they cannot take legal action like the Jews did.

Milkman contradicts Guitar's points by asserting the fact that there is no scientific data stating whites have a different genetic makeup. Calling Guitar crazy, Milkman points out that some whites have made great sacrifices for blacks. He then suggests Guitar follow Malcolm X's lead and change his name to Guitar X. When Guitar replies he doesn't care about names, Milkman says that Malcolm's point is to show whites that blacks do not have to accept their slave name. Guitar answers that the slave name does not bother him but slave status does.

In Chapter Seven, we turn to Milkman and Macon. Having spent his entire life under his father's roof, Milkman asks Macon if he can take leave for a year to focus on his personal ambitions. Although Macon resists and comes close to pleading with his son to stay, Milkman compares him to Pilate and her green sack hanging from the ceiling.

Suddenly, Macon is no longer interested in Milkman's departure but wants to know everything about the sack that supposedly contains Pilate's inheritance. He tells Milkman the story of what happened when his father died, this time not leaving any details out.

The narrative switches to a flashback. After the death of their father, Pilate and Macon find themselves homeless. Fortunately, they are rescued by Circe, the midwife who delivered them both; Circe hides them away in the mansion she works in right outside of Danville. Pilate and Milkman stay there for only two weeks, not able to bear the four walls closing in on them. Pilate pierces her ear and begins wearing her infamous earring constructed out of her mother's brass box. Once Pilate's ear heals, she and Macon escape to the joyous outdoors and have a ball. Soon, however, they are wandering around frightened with no definite plan of action until they see a ghost of their father motioning at the entrance of a cave. They spend the night there but in the morning Macon realizes they are not alone. Inside is an old white man. Scared, Macon kills him and discovers gold underneath the man's green blanket. Imagining a life of luxury, Macon plans on taking the gold with him until Pilate dissuades him, saying that taking the gold would look like a motive for killing the man. Pilate and Macon then begin to fight and Macon leaves the cave, and waits for Pilate to come out. Three days later, when the coast is free from hunters, he enters the cave only to find Pilate and the gold gone.

Macon becomes convinced that the green sack hanging in Pilate's house is the gold. As he licks his lips, he tells Macon to get the gold. If Milkman is able to get the gold, Macon tells him he can have half of it and can do whatever he wants.

Analysis

Guitar's anger at whites and desire to free blacks from oppression may be justified on a psychological level. Having to grow up poverty-stricken and watching his mother graciously accept forty dollars for her husband's dead body was instrumental in Guitar's growing dislike for whites. Even as a child, Guitar is ignored by a snotty white nurse who clearly considered blacks to be beneath her. However, Guitar's own reasoning in itself does not justify his actions. His belief that whites are unnatural and will all want to kill blacks for fun is absurd and scientifically untrue. Therefore, one can assume that his motive to kill whites is simply an act of revenge.

Ironically, Guitar's own actions can be considered "unnatural" as he exhibits traits of a serial killer. Guitar has already morphed into a reckless killer and we can that through his reply to Milkman. When Milkman asks if Guitar will one day kill him, Guitar answers that he doesn't kill Negroes. Milkman himself realizes that Guitar doesn't say he will not kill Milkman, but instead Negroes. This impersonal attitude towards another human being suggests Guitar is already become an out-of-control murderer.

The manner in which Chapter Six ends foreshadows the future outcome of Guitar's reckless attitude. When Milkman acknowledges he is afraid for Guitar, Guitar replies that he is afraid for Milkman, too. As there was no need for Guitar to be afraid for Milkman, his reply almost sounds like an ominous warning. Inharmoniously, Guitar's day is Sunday, a day in the Christian religion reserved for God and leisure.

Macon is obsessively intrigued by Pilate's sack, and tells Milkman the story of what happened after their father died. Interestingly, the story is not told in dialog, with Macon speaking, but is summarized by the narrator. Toni Morrison's decision may suggest that the narrator has an inner motive to tell the story. As objective as the narrator has been, one cannot assume that the narrator has summed up exactly what

Macon said. Therefore, the story about the gold in the cave may be unreliable.

Macon's pleading attitude in asking Milkman to go get the gold emphasizes his obsession with wealth. It has been over fifty years since Macon began believing his sister stole the gold, and he still has not forgiven her. Macon is blinded by his desire for money, and therefore cannot see that his pattern of thinking is illogical. One can assume that Pilate, a good and honest woman, would not have stolen the gold.

Summary and Analysis of Chapters 8 & 9

Summary

Guitar has to undertake a serious mission of bombing four white girls, in order to avenge four black girls that were bombed out of a church on a past Sunday. He realizes that he will need money to buy explosives, and his plans reach a dead end. Milkman arrives, and tells Guitar about his plan to steal the sack of gold from Pilate. In good humor once he learns of the potential money-making scheme, Guitar makes suggestions on how to rob Pilate's house. Both friends appear to be in great spirits as they fantasize about the possibilities so much money will bring.

While Guitar and Milkman saunter down Route Six they spot a white peacock on a roof of a low building. As they approach the building, the peacock flies down to strut in front of them. Guitar and Milkman attempt momentarily to catch the peacock before they once again start daydreaming about what they would do and buy with the money.

Though Milkman wants to steal the gold to get away from his family, he begins to have second doubts about robbing Pilate. Guitar, on the other hand, becomes insistent in going ahead with stealing the gold. Milkman, slightly dazed by Guitar's tone, does not think anything through but simply says he will pick Guitar up at one-thirty the following night.

The next night, both men enter Pilate's home through a window, cut the cord of the sack with a knife, and grab what they believe is the gold. As they are leaving, Milkman thinks he saw a silhouette of a man standing behind Guitar, but then decides it was the moonlight playing tricks on him. On the other side of the house, a woman stands at the window wondering what the thieves wanted the bag for.

In Chapter Nine, First Corinthians begins to secretly work as a maid, and tells her mother that she is an amanuensis to Michael-Mary Graham, the State Poet Laureate. After coming to the realization that she was a forty-two year old maker of rose petals, Corinthians suffers a great depression. She finally decides to find a job and be independent, but realizes that she has no useful skills even though she is well-traveled and a college graduate.

One day on her way to work, a man sits down next to her on the bus, and does so many times in the course of the next few weeks. Corinthians at first makes her disdain shown, but then, unexpectedly, she begins to be intrigued by this confident, elderly man. She soon falls in love with him. We find out that he is Henry Porter, a yardman and tenant of her father's. She is at first ashamed of dating him, and keeps their relationship a secret. Porter soon grows frustrated and calls her a "doll-baby." Corinthians soon sees the error of her ways and accompanies Porter to his home.

Sneaking into her room at four o'clock in the morning, just after leaving Porter's tiny rented room, Corinthians overhears her father and brother's loud discussion. As she hurries off to bed, Macon continues to insist that the gold must be in the cave. Milkman, though, is weary until he remembers being pulled over by the police for no reason. Angry for being thrown in jail, Macon reminds Milkman that he should be thankful he has a father with money.

Pilate eventually shows up at the police station to talk the police into releasing Milkman and Guitar, claiming that the bones they were arrested for belonged to her late husband, Mr. Solomon. On their way back from jail, Pilate tells Macon that she never took the gold, only the dead man's bones. Pilate claims after she left the cave, she saw her papa who told her that "if you take a life, you own it."

The next day, Milkman awakes to feel ashamed for stealing Pilate's sack. He decides to take a bath, still disgusted by the policeman searching him, and then realizes that his left leg is no longer shorter than his right one. Afterwards, he sets out to find Guitar, and accidentally comes across the gray Oldsmobile he oftentimes sees dropping Corinthians off at home. He notices Guitar outside the car sharing an intricate handshake with Railroad Tommy. Inside the car sit five other men, including Hospital Tommy, Porter, Empire State, Nero and one man unfamiliar to Milkman. Milkman quickly realizes that they are the Seven Days, and he is appalled that Corinthians is dating Porter. He goes home and informs his father, which leads to Corinthians having to quit her job, and Porter being evicted.

When Milkman comes home a little drunk, he is surprised to see Lena standing at the top of the stairs waiting for him. Lena is angry at Milkman's carefree and careless attitude, and accuses him of urinating all over her, Corinthians and Ruth all his life. Furious at Milkman for tattling on Corinthians, Lena slaps him, tells him he is exactly like Macon, and tells him the only reason he gets to decide what is best for them is because of the "hog's gut" that is in between his legs. Then, Lena informs him that she has stopped creating red velvet roses, and that he has urinated his last in their house.

Analysis

The white peacock Guitar and Milkman see is a symbol of their greed. The peacock dances in front of them and they want to catch it just as the image of the gold dances around in their minds and they want to find it. Macon Dead II also sees the white peacock's tail when he spots the gold in the cave. In some Asian cultures, the peacock is a symbol of wealth, while in others, it merely signifies beauty. However, both beauty and wealth are materialistic desires. The color white is associated with evil, and we can see an earlier example of white being negatively exposed through Freddie's tale of the white bull. In Christian tradition, the color white symbolizes purity, virginity and birth, but as a result of white oppression, the color takes on a sinister depiction.

Milkman's distress at being pulled over by the police for no apparent reason but his skin color ends his optimistic world view. This is the first time that he has experienced discrimination in his privileged life. Further agonizing is the fact that he if Macon Dead II had not been rich, Milkman would have stayed in jail. This experience draws Milkman closer to the rest of the African-American population, who at the time was being continuously discriminated against.

While the realization that both his legs are the same length does not appear to surprise Milkman, it signifies that he no longer is different from the rest of the black people. The fact that his skin color mattered more to the police than his money angered and upset him. It also unified him with the rest of his fellow African Americans. The prior limp and shorter leg were also signs of Milkman's lack of compassion. As soon as he finds himself ashamed for stealing from Pilate, he notices his legs are the same length.

Chapter Nine also brings about the transformation of Lena and Corinthian's characters. Usually classified as passive with no real life, they begin to revolt against the oppression in their own home. Corinthians takes a job as a maid to ensure her independence and ability to survive. She also takes on a lover from a lower social class. Lena, on the other hand, confronts Milkman with what he was his whole life, someone who uses but does not give back. Lena's decision to stop making fake roses suggests that she is no longer willing to live under false pretenses. Red imitation rose petals may also signify false love.

There is a conflict in the narrator's version of events with what Macon believes. The narrator claims that the gold is not in the cave but Macon believes it might still be there. The fact that the gold is not there when Milkman searches the cave suggests that the narrator is a more reliable source than Macon. However, sending Milkman on a wild goose chase is significant as his road to finding his identity is a long and twisted one.

Summary and Analysis of Chapter 10

Summary

Milkman informs Guitar of his plan to go look for the gold in the cave. By insisting that he should go to Montour County, Pennsylvania, by himself, Milkman arouses Guitar's suspicions that he might cheat him of the gold. Guitar reminds Milkman of how desperately he needs the money, firstly, to complete his Seven Days mission, and secondly, because Porter was evicted from his apartment on account of Macon.

After flying out to Pittsburgh, Milkman takes a Greyhound bus out to Danville, Pennsylvania. There, he locates the home of Reverend Cooper, an old time friend of his father's. Reverend Cooper, excited by Milkman's visit, exclaims that he knows Milkman's people, and then tells stories of Macon I and Macon II. Milkman feels a glow as he listens to Reverend Cooper, but is outraged when he hears that nothing was done to the Butlers, the people that killed his grandfather.

Reverend Cooper tells stories of Macon II working side by side with Macon I in the fields. Milkman then realizes that Macon II loved his father and had a personal relationship with him. Reverend Cooper reminisces about Macon I's cleverness and magnificence, declaring his farm was the most glorious for miles around. Milkman tells the reverend that Macon II is now a wealthy and successful man, and the reverend marvels at his ambition and good fortune.

The Butlers, a wealthy white family that owned the house that Circe had hidden them in as children, was now deceased, but Milkman decides to stop by the crumbling Butler estate anyways. As he enters the Butler mansion, Milkman is overwhelmed by a fierce rotting smell that changes into a spicy ginger fragrance. Inside, he sees a long hall that contains a spiral staircase, which he climbs. Atop the staircase stands an old woman with wild hair, everything in her face colorless except for the eyes and mouth. The woman is surrounded by dogs, savagely searching the apartment. She hugs him and is excited by his visit until she realizes that he is not Macon Dead II but his son. Milkman is unsure of who this woman is, and he compares her to dreams of witches he had in childhood.

Milkman discovers she is Circe, and she tells him what she knows about the Dead family history. Milkman learns that Macon Dead I's name was Jake and his wife's name was Sing. Milkman's grandmother, Sing, was believed to be a white lady, or perhaps Native American. Sing and Jake met on a wagon full of freed slaves going North from Charlemagne, Virginia. Circe also tells Milkman about Hunter's Cave, where Macon Dead I's body was dumped after it floated up from the river it was buried by. Allegedly claiming that he wanted to find his grandfather's bones to give him a proper burial, Milkman obtains directions to the cave. While taking his leave, he inquires as to why Circe remains in the mansion of her hated employers. Circe replies that she wants to make sure everything the Butlers stole and robbed to create their beautiful homes rots away to nothing. She also tells him that she has kept the dogs her mistress bred, and that they are helping her in destroying the estate.

Following the supposed scent of money through the overgrown farmland, Milkman falls into a creek and soaks his shoes, tears his clothes and destroys his expensive watch. He becomes agile in his pursuit once again, as his fixation to be a rich man returns. He finally makes it to the cave, and to his surprise, he finds nothing in it but leaves, boards and a tin can.

As soon as Milkman leaves the cave, he feels ravenous with hunger. He hitches a ride back to the Danville bus station, and after a meal consisting of six hamburgers, decides to go south to Virginia. In Virginia, Milkman believes, is where Pilate took her gold after she visited the cave. Milkman decides to follow her tracks, and perhaps someone who knows will tell him what happened to the gold.

Analysis

Milkman's trip to retrieve the gold is at first a proclamation of his selfish desires. The narrator describes him to be blinded by his desire for the gold, so much so that he does not analyze situations clearly. His idea to look for the gold in Virginia is illogical, and he seems to have lost all his sensibility. However, Milkman's reasons for wanting the gold are not as materialistic as they first appear. Milkman regards the gold as his only chance to escape his father's dominating character. The gold, therefore, serves as a means to create independence for Milkman.

Macon and Milkman each want the gold for different reasons. Macon's sole motivation is greed, his desire to accumulate profit. Milkman, on the other hand, is motivated by a desire to be independent. As Milkman continues in searching for the gold, his decision to go to Virginia is illogical. Perhaps unbeknown to him, Milkman chooses to go to Virginia in search of his character. On his way to Circe's dwelling, some of Milkman's material possessions are destroyed, signifying the desertion of his old identity.

Milkman's journey to Virginia soon becomes a blend of myth and reality. Milkman's encounter with Circe is apparently real to him, but leaves doubt in the minds of readers if a woman as old as Circe could still be living. Milkman, however, treats Circe as part of the realistic world, and it is she that gives him some information about his ancestry. Circe's namesake is not biblical but is taken from Homer's Odyssey. In the Odyssey, Circe is a sorceress who lives in a stone mansion in the woods. She also helps Odysseus find his way home. The Circe who Milkman encounters is also some type of an enchantress who aids him in finding his past.

The ruined Butler mansion alludes to the fact that money is only mortal. Once dead, the Butlers are forgotten and their mansion is purposely destroyed. The Butler mansion reiterates the concept of material wealth as being superficial and useless in many areas of life. The Butlers, who stole from others to make a profit, were dehumanized in the process. Macon, who watched his father die at the Butlers' hands, now shares some similarities with the aforementioned family. Both are numb to feeling as a result of constantly pursuing wealth. The last of Butlers, commits suicide after she discovers all the money is gone. Circe, as an act of revenge, allows dogs to destroy the house, a final insult.

The beginning of the chapter refers to the fairy tale of Hansel and Gretel, who must have felt such a craving for the gingerbread house that they became energized by their own hunger. An allusion to Milkman's reaction to when he first sees the cave, there is an ongoing aura of fantasy within Milkman's life. As he discovers there is no gold in the cave, that aura is broken. Milkman begins to realize that what he is looking for is not material in nature, but spiritual. Milkman's experience in the cave can be a reference to the biblical story of Jesus' resurrection. Also taking place in an empty cave, those who enter the cave at first do not realize that finding nothing can mean that there is something out there.

Summary and Analysis of Chapter 11

Summary

After several unsuccessful attempts to locate the town of Charlemagne, Milkman discovers it is actually called Shalimar. Milkman arrives in Shalimar, Virginia, and is astounded by the hospitable attitude in the South. He stops his car in front of Solomon's General Store, not out of choice but only because his fan belt broke, and purchases cherry-flavored soda inside. Inside, the owner informs Milkman that his friend had just been there looking for him. Milkman is surprised, even more so when he hears that Guitar left him a message of "your day is here." He soon comes to believe that Guitar is searching for him for professional reasons, as part of his Seven Days persona.

In order to clear his mind of the ominous threat left behind by Guitar, Milkman steps outside to rest on the store porch. Looking around, his eyes come to rest on a group of children standing in a circle and singing, "Jay the only son of Solomon..." He is drearily reminded of his childhood, and walks back inside in hopes of having his car fixed. Inside, he finds himself greeted by icy stares, and after a few heated words among the men, including one local named Saul, a fight breaks out. Milkman attempts to protect himself with a broken bottle but still endures a slashed wrist and a ripped suit.

Older men approach Milkman in order to challenge him to a new type of duel, one that would not involve fighting or knives. Instead, the chosen weapons are rifles, and the men all head out to Ryna's Gulch on a hunting trip. The men dress Milkman in military gear, stripping him of his nice suit. Milkman, a poor shot, hides his weakness and puts up a pretense of courage. The dark woods are intimidating, and it takes Milkman a while to fissure out how to differentiate between shadows and climb over rocks. Soon, Milkman hears a wailing sound similar to that of a woman crying. One of the men, Calvin, explains that it is only an echo and legend has it that a woman by the name of Ryna is crying in a nearby gulch, hence the name.

Soon, after what seems like miles and hours of walking, Milkman sits down to rest against a tree. Leaning back with his eyes closed, Milkman comes to the realization that he does not have endurance. His money and influential lineage are of no help to him in the forest. He then acknowledges that he has emotionally abused Hagar, his mother and father, and Pilate, solely for his own egocentric reasons.

Milkman snaps back into reality with the crackle of a wire in his ear. Guitar has found him and is repeatedly strangling him with a cord, chanting "your day has come". In the midst of struggling to catch a last dying breath, Milkman relaxes his body enough to give Guitar reason enough to believe he is dead. At that moment, he sees an image of Hagar bending over him "in perfect love." As Guitar loosens the cord, Milkman takes advantage of the situation long enough to shoot off his rifle into the trees ahead of him. Startled, Guitar loses his grasp on the wire and runs away into the woods.

Milkman finds the men just as they locate and shoot a bobcat. They finally remember to ask Milkman what he was shooting at earlier. Milkman lies and says he accidentally tripped and the gun went off. The men find Milkman's supposed lack of skill hilarious, and tease him about it all the way back to the car. Although having just escaped death, Milkman feels exhilarated and walks on the earth, without limping, like "he belonged on it."

The following day, the men meet in King Walker's gas station to discuss the events of the previous night. Over breakfast, Milkman discovers that his grandmother Sing's descendants still live in town. He also learns that Sing was an Indian, and that her mother's name was Heddy. Milkman decides to visit one of his family members who still lives in town, Susan Byrd. On his way to Susan's, Milkman stops and visits Sweet, a local prostitute, who bathes and makes love to him. Milkman returns her generosity by bathing her, making her bed and scouring her tub. Milkman gives her fifty dollars and tells her that he will come back again.

Analysis

In Chapter Eleven, Milkman undergoes a spiritual transformation. He is forced to reevaluate his life, and realizes he has been selfish in his treatment of Hagar and his parents. It then becomes clear to him that he has no endurance, and has relied on his money and impressive lineage for an edge. In the woods, his wealth and family background hinder him instead of help him. Also, whereas his money arouses respect in his home town, in Shalimar it inspires the locals to dislike him. The act of the men dressing Milkman up in military gear yet again signifies his transformation. Milkman is no longer a child spoiled by his luxurious upbringing but rather a man who can now fend for himself.

Milkman's metaphorical change goes hand in hand with his rebirth at the hands of his best friend, Guitar. As Guitar wrings the life out of Milkman through a wire, Milkman sees dancing lights and hears music, all the while he "had just drawn the last sweet air just left for him in the world." This suggestion that that Milkman dies is emphasized through his transformation. At that point in time, Milkman undergoes a rebirth because he survives his death to come back a changed man.

After his resurrection, Milkman acts like a different person. He now laughs with the rest of the men, and develops a camaraderie with them. As Chapter Eleven draws to a close, Milkman feels exhilarated to be walking the earth, and for the first time ever, he walks without a limp and feels as though he belongs. The limp, although imagined, acted as an emotional handicap for Milkman because it differentiated him from others. After his rebirth, Milkman no longer has the limp and now can join the rest of humanity.

Milkman first exhibits his compassionate side with Sweet, the local prostitute. Milkman's other acts of love were callous and egocentric, as he previously demonstrated with Hagar. Before, Milkman threw away Hagar's overwhelming love; now, accepts Sweet's passion and returns it by bathing her, making her bed, and scouring her tub. At the time of his metaphorical death, Milkman sees an image of Hagar bestowing upon him a perfect love. This image that flashes before his eyes represents Hagar's undying love and his rejection of it. This rejection, however, is overturned through his caring actions towards Sweet. Milkman has matured and understands now the importance of integrity and respect.

Throughout the novel, there has been an emphasis placed upon Milkman's last name, Dead. As Milkman often says himself, he can't die because he is already Dead. This wordplay is suggestive of his character and spiritual well-being. Prior to his rebirth, Milkman was dead in character. He has no endurance and no compassion. As he "dies" and is reborn, he is no longer Dead.

Summary and Analysis of Chapters 12 & 13

Summary

The following day, Milkman locates Susan Byrd's brick house and introduces himself. Reluctantly invited in, Milkman receives a warmer greeting from her friend, Grace Long. Although Susan Byrd is related to Sing, she claims that Sing was her aunt who left Virginia unmarried. Milkman is disappointed that his search has led him to a dead end, and hurriedly leaves Susan's home. Prior to leaving, however, Grace insists that he take some butter cookies with him, along with her address hidden inside the box.

On his way back to Shalimar, Milkman realizes that his family history is of great interest to him. Walking along, he finds Grace's address inside the box and smiles, until he notices that he left his gold watch back at Susan's house. Suddenly, he encounters Guitar leaning against a persimmon tree, waiting for him. Angry, Guitar accuses Milkman of finding the gold and shipping it to Virginia. Guitar is convinced of Milkman's betrayal, and claims that Milkman is trying to sabotage the Seven Days society. He promises to kill Milkman, but on his own schedule once he acquires the gold. Milkman realizes that he is not afraid but he is curious as to why Guitar would leave him a warning at Solomon's store. Guitar replies, "It's the least I could do for a friend."

Once again Milkman visits Sweet's home to sleep in her perfect arms. The following morning, he walks over to Solomon's store to have his car fixed. While waiting for King Walker, the man who was going to install his fan belt, Milkman takes a walk. He reflects on how silly it was to hate his family. He now feels homesick for Pilate, for his mother, for his father, and for his sisters. Milkman recognizes his mother's emotional and sexual starvation as part of who she is, and understands the depth of hurt she endures. He also begins to comprehend his father, a man who loved his own father, and who now showed his love by loving what his father died for: land. Milkman realizes that his father's love of property and wealth is a sign of grieving, of paying respect, to his own father, Macon Dead I. Most importantly, Milkman acknowledges the pain he caused Hagar, and feels ashamed of his actions.

All the while, he walks through the town, and notices that once again the children are playing some round games and singing that same song, "Solomon don't leave me here..." Paying closer attention to the lyrics, Milkman deciphers the words, and realizes that the song is about a man named Jake, who was raised by Heddy, and whose father's name was Solomon. Milkman excitedly realizes that the song talks about his family tree. He also comes to the conclusion that Susan Byrd gave him false information, and he decides to go visit her again.

In Chapter Thirteen, Guitar comes home to find Hagar standing listlessly in his room, thinking of Milkman. He drives her home, all the while telling her that she must not waste her life because of Milkman. During the car ride, Guitar tells Hagar how everything he loved in his life left him. He tells her of his father dying at age four, of his mother running away, of being raised by his grandmother and uncle, who are both near death now. Guitar mentions that because of all that, he now cannot commit to being in a relationship with a woman. And, the one time he did get involved with a woman, she deceived him. Yet Hagar pays no attention to his talk; her eyes are empty.

Hagar does not speak for several days. Pilate and Reba do everything to cheer her up but nothing works. Cooking special foods and buying presents does not wake Hagar up from her depressed trance. Then, one day, Pilate hands Hagar a pretty gold and pink compact, which Hagar peers into and sees her own reflection. She is suddenly struck by what must be the reason Milkman does not love her. She mutters, "No wonder," several times, and states that she is a mess. Hagar browses through her closet to discover that she has nothing to wear, and makes up her mind to go shopping.

Reba pawns her two thousand dollar diamond ring that she won for a mere two hundred dollars, and hands the money over to Hagar. Hagar goes on a shopping spree, buying everything from a garter belt to nylons to a slip. She then goes to the beauty salon, and emerges with a new hairdo. On her way home, Hagar is caught by a massive thunderstorm that destroys her new hairstyle and causes her shopping bags to rip open with their contents spilling onto the street. Hagar, though, is in an oblivious state and does not pay attention to anything surrounding her. She rushes home, and eagerly dresses herself in her new clothes. And yet, when she shows herself to Reba and Pilate, they are less than thrilled with her appearance. Hagar then sees that her hair is wild from the rain, that her pantyhose are ripped, and that her face make-up is clumpy. She begins to cry, and cries for so long that her eyes soon permanently dry up and she develops a high fever. In her delirium, Hagar cries about Milkman only liking wavy, penny-colored hair. After a few days, Hagar dies.

Pilate and Reba cannot afford a funeral because they spent their last dollars on getting Hagar what she wanted. It is Ruth who finally obtains the money from Macon. Few people attend the funeral. In the middle of the ceremony, Pilate enters the funeral home, followed by Reba, and they both begin to sing a hymn entitled, "Mercy." At the end of the ceremony, Pilate identifies Hagar as her baby girl, endlessly repeating the words for all the attendees. In the end, Pilate expresses her grief through proclaiming loudly to the skies, "And she was loved."

Analysis

Oral tradition plays an important role in the history of African Americans. During slavery, African Americans often included acting, gestures and singing into their storytelling, thereby creating it into an art. Storytelling also emphasizes repetition, rhythm and short phrases, making the story easily repeatable and memorable. Milkman discovers the importance of oral tradition when he realizes the meaning of the children's song/game. This also allows Milkman to come in direct contact with his roots, through an old African American tradition. Thus, Milkman finally accepts his black heritage.

The song of Solomon not only immortalizes Milkman's ancestry, it is also an important statement about African American social circumstances. In the song, Solomon abandons Ryna to fly back to Africa, and leaves her with twenty-one children. The theme of abandonment and flight is very prevalent throughout the entire novel. Guitar's mother flees after her husband's death, unable to bear the burden of raising her children alone. Pilate leaves behind Reba's father, lest he discover she does not have a navel. Milkman leaves behind Hagar, who bestowed upon him unconditional love. The theme of abandonment was also apparent in African American society; oftentimes, the male had to leave in order to search for work. Many times, as revealed through the Great Migration, families were torn apart as family members went North in search of work. Thus is the case with Milkman's family, as his father eventually traveled North and left his Southern homeland behind.

Hagar's death, indirectly caused by abandonment, has roots in her lack of a positive self-image. Hagar is convinced Milkman will love her if she changes her physical appearance, and so she goes on a wild shopping spree. Her plan does not work and Hagar dies believing Milkman would love her if she had silky, copper-colored hair. Hagar herself has kinky, at-times wild hair, and feels she does not meet the standards of beauty perpetuated by society, especially a white society. While she is dying, the narrator states she is in her Goldilocks bed, thereby making another reference to the fairy tale world. Hagar's death can also be compared to Sleeping Beauty's coma-like trance, who awaits her Prince Charming. Hagar however dies when she realizes Milkman will not come and rescue her with love.

Hagar's funeral is an odd ceremony when compared to typical African American funerals. Many African Americans believe that life is arduous, and that death allows for freedom. Most times, a reverend delivers words of comfort, and traditional hymns are sung. Pilate ignores ritual rites, enters halfway through the service, and sings a lullaby. Her indifference to tradition shows that she cannot be easily consoled, and also, it accentuates her independent character.

The final paragraphs of the chapter emphasize three colors, emerald, red, and black. All three colors evoke special significance, especially in the Christian religion. Green, a symbol of eternal life, shows hope that Hagar's soul will rest. Red carries connotations of fire and blood, as well as charity. Black signifies death.

Summary and Analysis of Chapters 14 & 15

Summary

Milkman revisits Susan Byrd, and pressures her into revealing all of his family history. Susan Byrd then tells him the story of his great-grandfather Solomon, who flew away from the plantation all the while carrying his son Jake with him. Solomon left behind his wife, Ryna, and all their twenty children except for Jake. During his flight, Solomon accidentally brushed against some tree branches and dropped his son Jake. Jake's fall was saved by the branches, and he landed in the backyard of an Indian woman named Heddy. Heddy had one child at the time, named Singing Bird, and decided to raise Jake as if he were her own. Soon after, Heddy gave birth to a boy named Crow Bird, later known as Crowell Byrd, who became Susan Byrd'd father. In the meantime, Sing had run off with Jake on a wagon full of freed slaves heading North.

Susan Byrd tells Milkman that she did not want to discuss her family history with Grace Long in the room because Grace has a bad habit of gossiping. Susan claims that if Grace found out Heddy didn't have a husband, it would be all over the county. Having rejected her black and Native American heritage, Susan is proud of having relatives who can pass for white. Her dislike for African Americans is clear when she refers to Jake as being black like coal. Prior to his leave, Milkman thanks Susan for all the information she was able to provide him, but he does not tell her he is a relative. Milkman thinks she would not be pleased to find out she has black relatives. He never does reclaim his gold watch.

Chapter Fifteen opens after Milkman leaves Susan Byrd's house. He rejoices at his newfound family history and arrives at Sweet's home, wanting to swim in the real sea. She and Milkman go to the local quarry, where they frolic around in the water. Milkman begins bellowing out the song of Solomon, much to Sweet's surprise.

Milkman finally begins his journey back to Michigan. He sells his car, which broke down again, and instead takes a bus. On the bus, Milkman ponders about the meanings of names, and thinks about his family both in the North and South. Suddenly Guitar's warning pops into his head, which forces Milkman to think about their ruined friendship. Milkman realizes that Guitar is to some degree insane but hopes he will be able to one day look past the gold, if he doesn't kill Milkman first.

In Michigan, Milkman visits Pilate. He is excited to share his discoveries with her. Instead of a big hug to welcome him back, Pilate hits him across the head with a wine bottle. Milkman wakes up to find himself in the cellar, surrounded by Hagar's things. He realizes that Hagar must be dead, and accepts this as his fault. Pilate believes that if someone takes a life, that life becomes whose ever took it. Precisely for that reason, Pilate has held onto the bones that she keeps in her green sack. After some time, Pilate enters the cellar and Milkman informs her that she has been carrying around her father's bones. He convinces her that she must bury him. Pilate then sends Milkman home with a boxful of Hagar's hair.

Upon his return home, he discovers that Corinthians has moved out with Porter and they now share a small house on the Southside. Lena, although still cold and unforgiving, is civil to him while his father and mother remain on the same terms. Macon is thrilled to hear about Milkman's trip to Virginia, and is especially proud to hear that places have been named after his family. Macon decides that he too one day will have to visit Virginia again.

Milkman and Pilate head out to Virginia to bury Macon Dead I's bones. They finally find a spot by a ravine called Solomon's Leap, and they dig a deep hole to bury the bones in. After the bones have been buried, Pilate takes off her earring and drops it into the grave. Just then, Pilate drops to the ground from a bullet destined for Milkman. Milkman takes her limp body in his hands and sings to her as she is dying.

Once he realizes that she is dead, Milkman gets up and screams Guitar's name. The mountains echo back a response, and in the shadows, Milkman sees Guitar's figure against the dark trees. Milkman then leaps into the air, and springs at Guitar. Milkman now knows that, "If you surrendered to the air, you could ride it."

Analysis

Susan Byrd's disdain for African-Americans and for Native Americans shows a lack of understanding at how rich her ancestry is. Instead of accepting her heritage, and therefore her past, Susan is only happy that her relatives are so light-skinned that they could pass for white. Interestingly, Susan is a teacher, but she does not want to learn anything about herself. As he is leaving, Milkman does not reclaim his gold watch, which Susan Byrd says Grace Long took. However, he is not at all affected by this news, thereby calling attention to his newfound lack of affection for material objects.

Pilate has carried her name in a snuffbox attached to her ear as a reminder of the importance of names. Once Milkman is aware of the history behind names, he gains a special knowledge that allows Pilate to take her name out of her ear. Pilate no longer needs her earring as a physical reminder as Milkman now has the spiritual and emotional knowledge to carry on their names to the next generation. Just as Pilate has carried her name as a physical memory, Milkman's family identity becomes an essential part of his identity.

The concept of flight not only begins the novel, but the story ends with it as well. Once dead, Pilate's body is encircled with birds, flying about her. One of the birds grabs the snuffbox out of the ground and carries it high in the air, signifying that Pilate's name and existence will live on through the generations. Milkman's belief in flight is reemphasized through his jump at Guitar. Morrison leaves Milkman's death in an ambiguous state, perhaps stating that whether he physically lives or not is not imperative. Milkman, who underwent a spiritual rebirth, will always be alive because his family name will now live on.

Milkman's final words emphasize not only his belief in flight, but his understanding of it. His ability to ride the air suggests that he has trust in the ability of how to choose his own fate. In contrast to the beginning of the novel where Mr. Smith fails at flight, we the readers are now presented with the possibility of a second chance. Milkman's jump at Guitar is optimistic as Milkman now understands how to fly. The concept of flight can be regarded as both realistic and hypothetical. Flight, throughout the entire novel, has been regarded as natural. After all, Solomon flew back to Africa. However, up until this point, no one has ever succeeded at flight. Milkman's spiritual rebirth as well as his newfound identity helps secure his survival against Guitar's revenge. However, it is up to the reader to decide whether or not Milkman wins over his opponent.

Suggested Essay Questions

1. Discuss the importance of names in reference to family history in *Song of Solomon*
2. Discuss the symbolic meaning of character names. Choose a minimum of two characters and research the meaning behind their names (e.g. Pilate, Hagar and/or Circe).
3. Analyze the possibility of flight in terms of pros and cons. How are escape and abandonment interrelated?
4. What does the color white signify in Song of Solomon? Use examples from the book to support your answer.
5. How does poverty affect Guitar's outlook on life? Could poverty have influenced his views on racial discrimination?
6. In Song of Solomon, do women face a double standard? Why or why not?
7. Research the Black Arts Movement. What key points from the Movement surface in this particular novel?
8. Why and how does Macon Dead II belive money is freedom?
9. Analyze the narrator's point of view. Are the narrator's views biased/unbiased?
10. Toni Morrison is renowned for her use of magical realism. Discuss the magical realism genre, then analyze how Morrison uses elements of this style.
11. Interpret the ending. Does Milkman survive Guitar's assassination attempt? How does he "ride the wind"?

Morrison's Folktale Source in Song of Solomon

Song of Solomon contains many allusions and references to both African and African American folktales and folk traditions, many of which are tied together by an interest in flying. Most obviously, the Angola legend of slaves who can fly out of bondage and back to Africa plays a crucial role in the beginning of the story and reappears at several points throughout. The tale was first collected by Langston Hughes and Arna Bontemps in their very influential work, *The Book of Negro Folklore*. As Naomi Von Tol notes in her essay, "The Fathers May Soar: Folklore and Blues in *Song of Solomon*," the Angola people whose descendents probably told this tale were widely regarded as possessing a special rapport with the supernatural. Their tales were cherished and preserved both by their own people and by other slave populations. Thus Morrison, in using the story, simultaneously continues this tradition of preserving the traditional tales and also enters into the parallel academic tradition of Hughes and Bontemps. In other words, she uses the folktale both as a creative artist and as a cultural historian. These two roles seem inextricably linked in her vision of African American heritage.

In the original tale, we are told that all Africans once had the power to fly, but that their wings were taken away due to their transgressions. However, some Africans retain this power, though their wings are not apparent and they look like anyone else. One day, a woman who has just given birth collapses in the fields from exhaustion. Her master beats her mercilessly. Upon a signal from the eldest slave, the woman escapes this beating by flying away suddenly. When the whites go after this elder, he too escapes, along with the rest of the slaves on the plantation, who fly away like a flock of crows, back to Africa. In this story, and in Morrison's novel, the sheer absurdity of African Americans' realities – the punishing economic and social conditions – lead to the embrace of a fantasy of flying. When reality grows too surreal to bear, such creative re-castings of one's powers may help to relieve the burden. Indeed, in this light, the whole of Morrison's creative effort might be likened to flight. We use the phrase "flight of fancy" to mean something frivolous; but a creative flight like Morrison's, and like Milkman's at the novel's end, captures a kind of catharsis out of despair that might be said to follow from the absurdities of the African American condition.

Author of ClassicNote and Sources

Anna Lis, author of ClassicNote. Completed on June 01, 2007, copyright held by GradeSaver.

Updated and revised W.C. Miller November 14, 2007. Copyright held by GradeSaver.

Century, Douglas. Toni Morrison. Philadelphia: Chelsea House, 1994.

Page, Philip. Dangerous Freedom: Fusion and Fragmentation in Toni Morrison's Novels. Jackson: University Press of Mississippi, 1996.

Willis, Susan. Specifying: Black Women Writing the American Experience. Madison: University of Wisconsin Press, 1987.

Jane Bakerman, "The Seams Can't Show: An Interview with Toni Morrison," Black American Literature Forum, 12 (1978): 56-60.

Colette Dowling, "The Song of Toni Morrison," New York Times Magazine, 20 May 1979, pp. 40, 42, 48, 52, 54, 56, 58.

Essay: Appreciation, Escape, and Resurrection

by Anonymous
September 01, 2002

In literature, what does it mean for somebody to fly? Ovid's Metamorphoses, chronicles of Greco-Roman mythology dating over 2000 years ago, depicts the failure of flight through the fates of Icarus and Phaeton, victims of hubris. Written by Toni Morrison and published in 1977, Song of Solomon opens and ends with the image of attempted flight. An array of paradoxical connotations emerges from this image such as triumph and failure, heroism and cowardice, and life and death. One can justify those dichotomies as a direct result to Morrison's decision to leave the reasoning behind Robert Smith and Milkman's leap into the air open to interpretation. Although it is unclear as to why Smith and Milkman attempt to fly, the readers discover the deterrent of flight through Milkman and Guitar's observation and interlocution about the grounded, ostentatious peacock. The conclusion is "the shit weighs you down" (179). To realize what it means to fly in this novel, this "shit" must be defined, as well. In Song of Solomon, images of flight reflect elements of past, present, and future: appreciation of one's origin, escape from societal domestication, and resurrection of the human spirit.

Whether it be a bird or plane, anything that can soar in the air must have its origin from the ground. Hence, before one can fly, one must be rooted. From the moment Milkman realizes that humans cannot fly, he detaches himself from the community as a consequence of this disheartening recognition. Although he befriends Guitar Bains, meets his enchanted aunt Pilate, and has coition with his cousin Hagar, Milkman is still aloof, for his desire to fly compels him to enervate and eventually abandon these human connections on the ground. When the Dead family's Packard rolls sedately through the city on Sunday afternoons, Milkman feels troubled because his sight is restricted to what he can see out of the rear window, illustrating Milkman's tragic flaw of depreciating the past in an attempt to catch a glimpse of what will pass. To watch the passing scenery he kneels on the seat, but "riding backward made him uneasy. It was like flying blind, and not knowing where he was going - just where he had been - troubled him" (32). The past should be one's cushion, not discomfort.

In a dream, Pilate sees her father and her father tells her, "You just can't fly on off and leave a body" (147). Jake's admonition suggests that one can only fly once all earthly affairs are resolved, for Pilate still has not interred the bones that she had been carrying for all those years. And only after Pilate buries her father's bones on Solomon's Leap can Pilate fly.

Milkman's odyssey to ascertain the origins of his name and family meets opposition with his conflicting desire to remain ignorant, for in ignorance he finds a superficial happiness and security. When Milkman is in the airplane for the first time in his life, the feeling of freedom he finds in the air is only a pale illusion, for Milkman still thinks freedom can be found only outside of reality and apart from his past. Milkman cannot fly without embracing his past as the air underneath his wings.

Raised by a man who talks black, lives white and thinks green, Milkman cannot see beyond the money, the house, and the Packard, for materialism and vanity is the "shit" that weighs him down from flying. For Milkman to truly fly, he must relinquish all that corrupts one's mind to disregard the values of identity and culture and instead embrace humanity. The peacock serves as the icon of societal domestication. Only once the peacock releases the heavy, ornate feathers on its tail will the peacock be able to soar freely without constraint. While belittling Pilate through his anecdote about the baby snake that eventually ate its caretaker, Macon Dead also teaches Milkman "the one important thing you'll ever need to know: Own things" (55). Macon Dead was not born into wealth, so he had to work with just ambition to reach the pinnacle of the black hierarchy; however, Milkman was born into wealth and took it for granted, which is even worse. Society corrupted Macon Dead's mind to such an extent that Macon Dead believes "money is freedom. The only real freedom there is" (163). Milkman adopts this principle, when he writes the word "gratitude" and includes money in a breakup letter to Hagar so that he can be liberated from Hagar's love. Money is not freedom or a liberator, especially in opposition to love. The laws of man may revolve around money but the statute of the skies does not acknowledge the value of materialism. As Milkman's journey develops and the layers of his family history begin to peel away, Milkman's money and possessions quickly become useless, for the fortune is not gold but rather the past and its people. "Without ever leaving the ground she could fly" because Pilate realized that no earthly possession held any value in her heart, which the reader learns through Pilate's disregard for her hair and social conventions (336). Milkman cannot fly until he strips off the weight of materialism and vanity on his back.

Although Robert Smith and Milkman leap into the air with no evidence of success, Pilate, even after her death, soars via the birds carrying her name in the air, which insinuates a spiritual resurrection. Death is not the end of the cycle for those whose spirits were pure. Resembling Christ's birth, life, and death, Pilate enters the world through her dead mother's womb unaided, carries the bones of her father as society condemns her a pariah, and dies with love as her last words for the sins of Milkman and Guitar's fatal ambition toward wealth. Yet she flies. Milkman regards Pilate's death as a graceful flight of freedom: "Now he knew why he loved her so. Without ever leaving the ground, she could fly" (336). Not only does Pilate resemble the life cycle of Christ, but she is an example of a human that came from the earth, for she is born without a bellybutton, eats what she grows, and is aware of her origins, which all contrast with Macon Dead, a man of society rather than earth. Robert Smith's letter about his scheduled flight from Mercy to Lake Superior bears resemblance to Christ's journey. His departure from Mercy connotes that Smith no longer wanted to be at the mercy of society, so he flew to Lake Superior, the symbol of haven or even heaven. Convicted for claiming to be the Son of God, Christ did not receive

Essay: Appreciation, Escape, and Resurrection

clemency from the throng of Jewish people and eventually was crucified, but He did rise from the dead and ascended to heaven. Hence, flight can be perceived as resurrection. After Guitar murders Pilate, Milkman realizes that only in death will Milkman be able to rise from the dead and fly like Solomon and Pilate, so he asks Guitar, "You want my life? You need it? Here" (337). He leaps off the cliff. Milkman realizes that "if you surrendered to the air, you could ride it" (337). Pilate's rooted flight arises out of her true knowledge and recognition of the entangled feelings of love, animosity, faith, and anguish that define the existence of herself and her people; embracing the contradictions of humanity allows Pilate to live and die in joyful freedom. Seeking this freedom, Milkman takes flight at last.

If one attempts to fly solo without human connections, without knowledge of the past, and without true love, then not only is that one capable of killing others but also one's identity and culture. In order for Milkman to see the future, he must recognize, recollect, and reconcile himself to the past. Staring death, via Guitar, in its catlike eyes, Milkman gives everything for love, knowing that love is not a burden or oppression but freedom. Although the final image of flight in Song of Solomon lacks a definitive conclusion, one must not mettle with the question of whether he lives or dies, but rather whether he dies or flies.

Essay: Appreciation, Escape, and Resurrection

Quiz 1

1. **What are the names of Macon Dead II's children?**
   A. Macon Dead III, Mary, and Magdalene
   B. Macon Dead III, First Corinthians, and Magdalene
   C. Macon Dead III, Mary, and Hagar
   D. Macon Dead III, First Corinthians, and Hagar

2. **What is the name of Milkman's aunt?**
   A. Pilate
   B. Rebecca
   C. Mary
   D. Hagar

3. **Where was Macon Dead I's farm located?**
   A. Washington County, Massachusetts
   B. Lincoln County, Pennsylvania
   C. Montour County, Pennsylvania
   D. Lincoln County, Virginia

4. **What is the name of Pilate's daughter?**
   A. Reba
   B. Lena
   C. Mary
   D. Hagar

5. **What was Ruth's father's profession?**
   A. Doctor
   B. Lawyer
   C. Bartender
   D. Professor

6. **Where was Milkman born?**
   A. At home
   B. At Pilate's house
   C. At No Mercy Hospital
   D. In the fields

7. **What does Pilate's earring contain?**
    A. Her father's gold teeth
    B. A silver coin from the Civil War
    C. A section of her mother's gold necklace
    D. A bible page with her name

8. **How did Macon Dead I die?**
    A. He was shot while defending his land
    B. He fell sick during the great migration
    C. He was murdered by his wife
    D. He just disappeared

9. **What did Reba win from Sears for being the 500,000th customer?**
    A. A diamond ring
    B. A lifetime supply of hair products
    C. A hundred pounds of groceries
    D. A yearly subscription to Wall street

10. **Why was Milkman refused entry into Feather's pool hall?**
    A. Feather did not like Milkman' father
    B. Feather said he was too young
    C. Milkman's mother had once insulted Feather
    D. He was loud and disrespectful

11. **Pilate was born without...**
    A. Body Hair
    B. A left pinkie toe
    C. An Ear
    D. A navel

12. **Why did Milkman physically assault his father at the dinner table?**
    A. Macon punched Ruth in the jaw
    B. Macon slapped First Corinthians across the cheek
    C. Milkman was under the influence of marijuana and alcohol
    D. Macon threw a plate at him

13. **Macon finds Ruth sexually repulsive because...**
   A. She cheated on him with Porter
   B. He thinks she had an affair with her own father
   C. He does not think Milkman is his own child
   D. He became devoted to money and lost all interest in sex

14. **What woman tries to repeatedly kill Milkman and why?**
   A. Hagar; she is mad because Milkman does not love her
   B. First Corinthians; Milkman killed her lover and she is seeking
revenge
   C. Pilate; Milkman betrayed her by stealing her money
   D. Lena; she suffers from delusions

15. **Who owns the barbershop Milkman and Guitar frequent?**
   A. Pilate
   B. Hospital Tommy and Railroad Tommy
   C. Feather
   D. Driver Tommy and Railroad Tommy

16. **Why does Ruth confront Hagar?**
   A. Hagar tried to seduce Ruth's husband, Macon
   B. Ruth does not confront Hagar
   C. Hagar has been spreading vicious rumors about Ruth
   D. Hagar has been unsuccessfully trying to kill her son

17. **Who first informs Milkman of Guitar's activities?**
   A. Pilate
   B. Porter
   C. Freddie
   D. Macon

18. **What is Honore?**
   A. The name of a blue Ford Porter drives
   B. A lake with beach houses
   C. Guitar's secret code name
   D. Reba's father's name

19. **What religion is Ruth?**
    A. Episcopalian
    B. Catholic
    C. Orthodox
    D. Methodist

20. **What society does Guitar belong to?**
    A. Seven Night Klan
    B. Night Klan
    C. Seven Days
    D. Seven Nights

21. **Who is Circe?**
    A. A midwife who hid Pilate and Macon after their father was killed
    B. There is no one in the book by that name
    C. Macon Dead III's wife's name
    D. A temperamental co-worker that First Corinthians befriends

22. **What did Macon and Pilate encounter in the cave?**
    A. The remains of their mother
    B. Two dead men and a container of silver coins
    C. A old man and gold
    D. The cave was empty

23. **What type of car did Macon Dead II own?**
    A. A green Packard
    B. A black Chevrolet
    C. A black Ford
    D. A green Ford

24. **What does First Corinthians do after she suffers a severe depression at the age of forty-two?**
    A. Begins to visit bars
    B. Finds a job as a maid
    C. Disappears
    D. Goes back to college

25. **First Corinthians is at first reluctant to engage in a relationship with Porter because:**
    A. She finds Porter repulsive
    B. She is traumatized by the lack of love in her home
    C. She already has another love interest
    D. She is scared of her father

Quiz 1 Answer Key

1. (**B**) Macon Dead III, First Corinthians, and Magdalene
2. (**A**) Pilate
3. (**C**) Montour County, Pennsylvania
4. (**A**) Reba
5. (**A**) Doctor
6. (**C**) At No Mercy Hospital
7. (**D**) A bible page with her name
8. (**A**) He was shot while defending his land
9. (**A**) A diamond ring
10. (**A**) Feather did not like Milkman' father
11. (**D**) A navel
12. (**A**) Macon punched Ruth in the jaw
13. (**B**) He thinks she had an affair with her own father
14. (**A**) Hagar; she is mad because Milkman does not love her
15. (**B**) Hospital Tommy and Railroad Tommy
16. (**D**) Hagar has been unsuccessfully trying to kill her son
17. (**C**) Freddie
18. (**B**) A lake with beach houses
19. (**D**) Methodist
20. (**C**) Seven Days
21. (**A**) A midwife who hid Pilate and Macon after their father was killed
22. (**C**) A old man and gold
23. (**A**) A green Packard
24. (**B**) Finds a job as a maid
25. (**D**) She is scared of her father

Quiz 2

1. **How does Pilate die?**
   A. She is accidentally shot by Guitar.
   B. She is murdered by Circe.
   C. She dies of a broken heart.
   D. Macon Dead II strangles her.

2. **Who is Sweet?**
   A. Hagar's cousin
   B. Reverend Cooper's wife
   C. A prostitute
   D. Guitar's girlfriend

3. **Sing's original name was...**
   A. Sing Love
   B. Sarah
   C. Sighing Bird
   D. Singing bird

4. **Where did Solomon fly off to?**
   A. the North
   B. the South
   C. Haiti
   D. Africa

5. **Who is Ryna?**
   A. Heddy's mother
   B. Solomon's wife
   C. Pilate's friend
   D. Guitar's mother

6. **The white peacock symbolizes:**
   A. Hatred
   B. Virtue
   C. Gluttony
   D. Greed

7. **Robert Smith was**
>   A. a professor at the college First Corinthians attended
>   B. Ruth's father
>   C. an insurance agent and a member of the Seven Days
>   D. an alcoholic who raped Lena

8. **Guitar tries to kill Milkman because...**
>   A. He thinks Milkman is plotting to kill him
>   B. He is convinced Milkman cheated him out of the gold
>   C. Guitar is not trying to kill Milkman
>   D. He hates the fact that Milkman is rich

9. **Whose bones were in Pilate's green sack?**
>   A. Her uncle's
>   B. Her father's
>   C. Her mother's
>   D. Her dead son's

10. **Who is Reverend Cooper?**
>   A. The man who forces Milkman to see the light
>   B. A member of the Seven Days society
>   C. Ruth's pastor at her church
>   D. An old acquaintance of Macon Dead II

11. **Who takes Milkman's gold watch?**
>   A. Grace Long
>   B. Susan Byrd
>   C. Ryna
>   D. Sweet

12. **How does Guitar try to kill Milkman?**
>   A. Through poison
>   B. With a gun
>   C. By strangulation
>   D. With a knife

13. **Who does Corinthians engage in a romantic relationship with?**
    A. Porter
    B. Freddie
    C. Feather
    D. Railroad Tommy

14. **Porter works as a:**
    A. yardman
    B. janitor
    C. engineer
    D. bartender

15. **Who raises Jake?**
    A. Pilate
    B. Susan Byrd
    C. Heddy
    D. Singing Bird

16. **Why was Jake raised by Heddy?**
    A. Jake never knew his parents.
    B. Ryna disowned him.
    C. Jake's mother died when he was just a boy.
    D. Solomon dropped him in front of her home.

17. **How did the Dead family obtain their name?**
    A. Through a clerical mistake
    B. "Dead" refers to their hometown
    C. A fortuneteller predicted it would bring the family luck
    D. From their master

18. **What is Milkman's great-grandfather's name?**
    A. Solomon
    B. Dr. Foster
    C. Macon Dead I
    D. Jake

19. **Flight can be associated with:**
    A. Hatred
    B. Virtue
    C. Love
    D. Escape

20. **Guitar harbors a hatred for:**
    A. Whites
    B. Rich people
    C. Poor people
    D. Blacks

21. **Hagar is convinced she can win Milkman's love by...**
    A. undergoing a complete physical make-over
    B. hurting herself physically
    C. confessing her true feelings for him
    D. killing his mother

22. **What did Guitar's mother recieve for his father's body?**
    A. A free funeral
    B. Four ten dollar bills
    C. Life insurance worth fifty dollars
    D. Life insurance worth three hundred dollars

23. **Who is Guitar's love interest?**
    A. Guitar does not have a love interest
    B. Marcelline
    C. Hagar
    D. Michael-Mary Graham

24. **Who does First Corinthians work for?**
    A. Reverend Cooper
    B. Mary Studebaker
    C. Macon Dead II
    D. Michael-Mary Graham

25. No Mercy Hospital derived its' name from:

A. The ironic name of the hospital's founder

B. Its' refusal to admit blacks

C. Its' disbelief in anesthesia

D. The excessive amount of deaths that occur yearly

Quiz 2 Answer Key

1. **(A)** She is accidentally shot by Guitar.
2. **(C)** A prostitute
3. **(D)** Singing bird
4. **(D)** Africa
5. **(B)** Solomon's wife
6. **(D)** Greed
7. **(C)** an insurance agent and a member of the Seven Days
8. **(B)** He is convinced Milkman cheated him out of the gold
9. **(B)** Her father's
10. **(D)** An old acquaintance of Macon Dead II
11. **(A)** Grace Long
12. **(B)** With a gun
13. **(A)** Porter
14. **(A)** yardman
15. **(C)** Heddy
16. **(D)** Solomon dropped him in front of her home.
17. **(A)** Through a clerical mistake
18. **(A)** Solomon
19. **(D)** Escape
20. **(A)** Whites
21. **(A)** undergoing a complete physical make-over
22. **(B)** Four ten dollar bills
23. **(A)** Guitar does not have a love interest
24. **(D)** Michael-Mary Graham
25. **(B)** Its' refusal to admit blacks

Quiz 3

1. **What is Rebecca's nickname?**
    A. "B"
    B. Reba
    C. Hagar
    D. Becky

2. **What does Susan Byrd tell Milkman?**
    A. She surprises him by stating she knew Macon Dead II
    B. She informs him of his ancestors' names and their history
    C. She warns him of Guitar's plan to kill him
    D. She tells him blacks are not allowed in her home

3. **Why is Pilate's home referred to as a "wine-house"?**
    A. Reba is constantly sneaking wine into the house
    B. Pilate enjoys drinking wine at home
    C. As a teenager, Hagar would get drunk from wine
    D. Pilate supports herself financially by making wine

4. **What drives Macon to accumulate wealth and land?**
    A. He wants to show Pilate he is better than her
    B. He emotionally strives to accumulate what his father died for: property.
    C. He desires to be as well known as Ruth's father, Dr. Foster
    D. He needs money to support his drug habit

5. **As an adolescent, why does Milkman enjoy working for his father?**
    A. His father pays him well
    B. He is now able to see his girlfriend every day
    C. He is excused from school
    D. He gets to visit the Southside and spend time with his buddy Guitar

6. **Where is the Blood Bank area located?**
    A. In Shalimar, Virginia
    B. On the East Side of town
    C. In Honore
    D. In the Southside

7. **Where does Milkman's spiritual rebirth occur?**
    A. In the cave in Pennsylvania
    B. At Sweet's home
    C. In a forest in Shalimar
    D. At Pilate's house

8. **Why does Guitar want the gold so badly?**
    A. He becomes obsessed with accumulating wealth, like Macon
    B. He wants to to buy a house
    C. He needs it to complete his Seven Days mission
    D. He thinks it will help him in attracting women

9. **How many children did Solomon leave behind?**
    A. Twelve
    B. Twenty
    C. Two
    D. Twenty-One

10. **What nationality was Heddy?**
    A. African
    B. Mexican
    C. Irish-American
    D. Native-American

11. **Who develops a slight infatuation with Milkman?**
    A. Grace Long
    B. Reba
    C. Marcelline
    D. Michael-Mary Graham

12. **Why does Lena slap Milkman?**
    A. He tried pushing her down the stairs
    B. She is upset that he burglarized Pilate's home
    C. She discovers he has an alcohol problem
    D. She is tired of his egocentric and inconsiderate ways

13. Where does Macon discover gold?

  A. In Pilate's home

  B. In the Butler's mansion

  C. In the cave

  D. In the forest

14. Who are the Butlers?

  A. A rich, white family who killed for land and money

  B. The family that adopted Macon and Pilate after their father died

  C. Ruth Foster's maternal cousins

  D. Circe's godparents

15. What does Ruth state at the dinner table that infuriates Macon?

  A. She says she is her "daddy's daughter"

  B. She proclaims she is blessed

  C. She swears that she will "kill Milkman"

  D. She admits she does not love her husband

16. What suggests that Susan Byrd is ashamed of her heritage?

  A. She claims her family is Irish

  B. She refuses to acknowlege her Native-American roots

  C. She admits to lightening her hair color

  D. She is proud to have relatives that can pass for white

17. What does Pilate give Milkman as a reminder of Hagar's death?

  A. A box filled with Hagar's hair

  B. Her earring containing Hagar's name

  C. A bottle of Hagar's favorite perfume

  D. A snuffbox with Hagar's eyelashes

18. How many mourners attend Hagar's funeral?

  A. The funeral parlor is empty

  B. All the Southside residents

  C. About two dozen

  D. A handful

19. **What does Ruth do when she leaves the house late at night?**
    A. She has an affair with Porter
    B. She visits Pilate to talk about her failed marriage
    C. She visits her father's grave at the cemetary
    D. She meets with an old friend named Miller

20. **Why does Saul pick a fight with milkman?**
    A. Milkman points a gun at Saul's friend Chase
    B. Saul is offended by Milkman's big-city ways
    C. Saul thinks Milkman is trying to steal his money
    D. Milkman unintentionally insults Saul's wife

21. **Milkman's relationship with Sweet can be described as:**
    A. Vulgar
    B. Intentionally cruel
    C. Mutually respectful
    D. Egocentric

22. **Why does Ruth confront Hagar?**
    A. Ruth resents the fact that Hagar is trying to kill her Milkman
    B. Hagar vandalized Ruth's house
    C. Ruth is jealous of Hagar's beauty
    D. Hagar accidentally stabbed First Corinthians

23. **How many sisters does Milkman have?**
    A. Two
    B. Twenty-One
    C. Five
    D. Three

24. **As Milkman enters the crumbling Butler mansion, what is he overwhelmed by?**
    A. The dead animals
    B. The rotting smell
    C. The site of the destroyed chapel
    D. The beautiful sculptures

25. **What is the name of the gold-filled cave?**
   A. Jake's Cave
   B. Circe's Cave
   C. Cooper's Cave
   D. Hunter's Cave

Quiz 3 Answer Key

1. **(B)** Reba
2. **(B)** She informs him of his ancestors' names and their history
3. **(D)** Pilate supports herself financially by making wine
4. **(B)** He emotionally strives to accumulate what his father died for: property.
5. **(D)** He gets to visit the Southside and spend time with his buddy Guitar
6. **(D)** In the Southside
7. **(C)** In a forest in Shalimar
8. **(C)** He needs it to complete his Seven Days mission
9. **(D)** Twenty-One
10. **(D)** Native-American
11. **(A)** Grace Long
12. **(D)** She is tired of his egocentric and inconsiderate ways
13. **(C)** In the cave
14. **(A)** A rich, white family who killed for land and money
15. **(A)** She says she is her "daddy's daughter"
16. **(D)** She is proud to have relatives that can pass for white
17. **(A)** A box filled with Hagar's hair
18. **(D)** A handful
19. **(C)** She visits her father's grave at the cemetary
20. **(B)** Saul is offended by Milkman's big-city ways
21. **(C)** Mutually respectful
22. **(A)** Ruth resents the fact that Hagar is trying to kill her Milkman
23. **(A)** Two
24. **(B)** The rotting smell
25. **(D)** Hunter's Cave

Quiz 4

1. **What does Milkman learn about his father from Reverand Cooper?**
    A. Macon was secretly relieved when his mother died
    B. Macon was a compassionate man who loved his father
    C. Macon always had a strong dislike for Pilate
    D. In his early age, Macon was disrespectful to the townspeople

2. **Who leaves Milkman a message of "your day is here"?**
    A. Guitar
    B. Porter
    C. Reverend Cooper
    D. Lena

3. **Who is Ryna's Gulch named after?**
    A. Sweet's mother
    B. Milkman's great-grandmother
    C. Saul's wife
    D. Susan Byrd's mother

4. **What type of a duel do the elders of Shalimar challenge Milkman with?**
    A. A hunting trip
    B. A car race
    C. A gun fight
    D. A wrestling match

5. **How does Milkman tell Hagar that he does not want her?**
    A. Inside a church, with the pastor preaching
    B. In Pilate's home, while Reba is singing
    C. He asks Guitar to tell her he doesn't love her
    D. Through a letter, signed with gratitude

6. **Where did Freddie spend his childhood?**
    A. On train wagons
    B. In a jailhouse - he was an orphan
    C. At the local church - his family abandoned him
    D. Working on a plantation

7. **Freddie's story about his mother's daeth involves which animal?**
    A. A white peacock
    B. A black bull
    C. A black wolf
    D. A white bull

8. **What does Guitar believe Milkman did with the gold?**
    A. He thinks Milkman traded it for greenbacks
    B. He believes Milkman hid it in Shalimar
    C. He believes Milkman gave it to his father
    D. He thinks Milkman shipped it to Virginia

9. **In Chapter Six, what African-American leader does Milkman make a reference to?**
    A. Malcolm X
    B. Martin Luther King
    C. Booker T Washington
    D. De Bois

10. **As a member of the Seven Days, what is Guitar's day?**
    A. Friday
    B. Monday
    C. Sunday
    D. Saturday

11. **the Seven days society consists of how many members?**
    A. Fourteen
    B. Four
    C. Eight
    D. Seven

12. **What does Milkman believe is wrong with him physically?**
    A. His smile is lopsided
    B. He has a lazy eye
    C. His right hand is a lot smaller than his left
    D. His left leg is shorter than the right

13. **Which of the following women have been abandoned?**
    A. Ruth and Hagar
    B. Pilate and Ryna
    C. Pilate and Ruth
    D. Ryna and Hagar

14. **Milkman's egocentric attitude is apparent through...**
    A. His relationship with Sweet
    B. His treatment of Hagar
    C. His pursuit of the gold
    D. His interest in his family background

15. **Pilate takes her earring off because...**
    A. It was weighing down her ear
    B. Her granddaughter died
    C. She knows her name will live on
    D. She loses faith in her family history

16. **The birds flying over Pilate's body are yet another example of:**
    A. an evil spirit
    B. a departed soul
    C. The themes of greed and hunger
    D. The theme of flight

17. **In the end, what suggests Milkman's belief in flight?**
    A. His grief over Pilate's death
    B. The discovery of his family history
    C. His anger at Hagar's death
    D. His jump at Guitar

18. **What demonstrates Lena's independent personality?**
    A. Her jealousy of Corinthian's relationship with Porter
    B. Her angry criticism of Milkman's attitude
    C. Her lack of desire to create red velevet roses
    D. Her reproachful attitude towards her father

19. **What is an example of magic realism in the novel?**
    A. Guitar mistakenly shooting Pilate instead of Milkman
    B. Robert Smith's fateful flight
    C. Reverend Cooper's admiration for Macon Dead II
    D. The tulip bulbs suffocating Ruth

20. **In the novel, what does the color white signify?**
    A. Hatred
    B. Good
    C. Hope
    D. Evil

21. **Why was Ruth was the first black woman admitted to No Mercy hospital?**
    A. She was overlooked in the commotion surrounding Robert Smith's death
    B. Because her father was the first black doctor in town
    C. The hospital wanted to make a statement
    D. She was able to afford the stay because of Macon's money

22. **What influenced Guitar's hatred of whites?**
    A. His rejection by a white woman
    B. His mother's jealous attitude
    C. His genetic make-up, or so he claims
    D. His father's death and his poverty

23. **Hagar's name is**
    A. An example of magical realism
    B. A reference to The Odyssey
    C. The author's imagination at work
    D. A biblical allusion

24. **What happens to Milkman at the end of the book?**
    A. Guitar shoots him and he dies
    B. He kills himself
    C. It is up to the reader to make his/her own conclusions
    D. He runs away from Guitar and lives

25. What is Toni Morrison's given name?
A. Chloe Anthoney Wofford
B. Harriet Woodson
C. Toni Clark
D. Ruth Maria Sterling

Quiz 4 Answer Key

1. (**B**) Macon was a compassionate man who loved his father
2. (**A**) Guitar
3. (**B**) Milkman's great-grandmother
4. (**A**) A hunting trip
5. (**D**) Through a letter, signed with gratitude
6. (**B**) In a jailhouse - he was an orphan
7. (**D**) A white bull
8. (**D**) He thinks Milkman shipped it to Virginia
9. (**A**) Malcolm X
10. (**C**) Sunday
11. (**D**) Seven
12. (**D**) His left leg is shorter than the right
13. (**D**) Ryna and Hagar
14. (**B**) His treatment of Hagar
15. (**C**) She knows her name will live on
16. (**D**) The theme of flight
17. (**D**) His jump at Guitar
18. (**B**) Her angry criticism of Milkman's attitude
19. (**D**) The tulip bulbs suffocating Ruth
20. (**D**) Evil
21. (**A**) She was overlooked in the commotion surrounding Robert Smith's death
22. (**D**) His father's death and his poverty
23. (**D**) A biblical allusion
24. (**C**) It is up to the reader to make his/her own conclusions
25. (**A**) Chloe Anthoney Wofford

ClassicNotes

GradeSaver™

Getting you the grade since 1999™

Other ClassicNotes from GradeSaver™

1984
Absalom, Absalom
Adam Bede
The Adventures of Augie March
The Adventures of Huckleberry Finn
The Adventures of Tom Sawyer
The Aeneid
Agamemnon
The Age of Innocence
Alice in Wonderland
All My Sons
All Quiet on the Western Front
All the King's Men
All the Pretty Horses
The Ambassadors
American Beauty
Angela's Ashes
Animal Farm
Anna Karenina
Antigone
Antony and Cleopatra
Aristotle's Ethics
Aristotle's Poetics
Aristotle's Politics
As I Lay Dying
As You Like It
Astrophil and Stella
The Awakening
Babbitt
The Bacchae
Bartleby the Scrivener
The Bean Trees

The Bell Jar
Beloved
Benito Cereno
Beowulf
Bhagavad-Gita
Billy Budd
Black Boy
Bleak House
The Bloody Chamber
Bluest Eye
The Bonfire of the Vanities
Brave New World
Breakfast at Tiffany's
The Brothers Karamazov
Call of the Wild
Candide
The Canterbury Tales
Cat's Cradle
Catch-22
The Catcher in the Rye
The Caucasian Chalk Circle
The Cherry Orchard
The Chosen
A Christmas Carol
Chronicle of a Death Foretold
Civil Disobedience
Civilization and Its Discontents
A Clockwork Orange
The Color of Water
The Color Purple
Comedy of Errors
Communist Manifesto

A Confederacy of Dunces
Confessions
Connecticut Yankee in King Arthur's Court
The Consolation of Philosophy
Coriolanus
The Count of Monte Cristo
Crime and Punishment
The Crucible
Cry, the Beloved Country
The Crying of Lot 49
Cymbeline
Daisy Miller
Death in Venice
Death of a Salesman
The Death of Ivan Ilych
Democracy in America
Devil in a Blue Dress
Dharma Bums
The Diary of Anne Frank
Disgrace
Divine Comedy-I: Inferno
A Doll's House
Don Quixote Book I
Don Quixote Book II
Dr. Faustus
Dr. Jekyll and Mr. Hyde
Dracula
Dubliners
East of Eden
Emma

For our full list of over 250 Study Guides, Quizzes,
Sample College Application Essays, Literature Essays and E-texts, visit:

www.gradesaver.com

ClassicNotes

GrAdeSaver™

Getting you the grade since 1999™

Other ClassicNotes from GradeSaver™

Ender's Game
Endgame
The English Patient
Ethan Frome
The Eumenides
Everything is Illuminated
Fahrenheit 451
The Fall of the House of
  Usher
Farewell to Arms
The Federalist Papers
For Whom the Bell Tolls
The Fountainhead
Frankenstein
Franny and Zooey
Glass Menagerie
The God of Small Things
The Good Earth
The Grapes of Wrath
Great Expectations
The Great Gatsby
The Guest
Gulliver's Travels
Hamlet
The Handmaid's Tale
Hard Times
Heart of Darkness
Hedda Gabler
Henry IV (Pirandello)
Henry IV Part 1
Henry IV Part 2
Henry V
Herzog
The Hobbit
Homo Faber
House of Mirth

House of the Seven
  Gables
The House of the Spirits
House on Mango Street
Howards End
A Hunger Artist
I Know Why the Caged
  Bird Sings
An Ideal Husband
Iliad
The Importance of Being
  Earnest
In Our Time
Inherit the Wind
Invisible Man
The Island of Dr. Moreau
Jane Eyre
Jazz
The Jew of Malta
The Joy Luck Club
Julius Caesar
Jungle of Cities
Kama Sutra
Kidnapped
King Lear
The Kite Runner
Last of the Mohicans
Leviathan
Libation Bearers
Life is Beautiful
Light In August
The Lion, the Witch and
  the Wardrobe
Lolita
Long Day's Journey Into
  Night

Lord Jim
Lord of the Flies
The Lord of the Rings:
  The Fellowship of the
  Ring
The Lord of the Rings:
  The Return of the
  King
The Lord of the Rings:
  The Two Towers
A Lost Lady
Love in the Time of
  Cholera
The Love Song of J.
  Alfred Prufrock
Lucy
Macbeth
Madame Bovary
Manhattan Transfer
Mansfield Park
MAUS
The Mayor of
  Casterbridge
Measure for Measure
Medea
Merchant of Venice
Metamorphoses
The Metamorphosis
Middlemarch
Midsummer Night's
  Dream
Moby Dick
Moll Flanders
Mother Courage and Her
  Children
Mrs. Dalloway

For our full list of over 250 Study Guides, Quizzes,
Sample College Application Essays, Literature Essays and E-texts, visit:

www.gradesaver.com

ClassicNotes

GradeSaver™

Getting you the grade since 1999™

Other ClassicNotes from GradeSaver™

Much Ado About
   Nothing
My Antonia
Native Son
Night
No Exit
Notes from Underground
O Pioneers
The Odyssey
Oedipus Rex / Oedipus
   the King
Of Mice and Men
The Old Man and the Sea
On Liberty
On the Road
One Day in the Life of
   Ivan Denisovich
One Flew Over the
   Cuckoo's Nest
One Hundred Years of
   Solitude
Oroonoko
Othello
Our Town
Pale Fire
Paradise Lost
A Passage to India
The Pearl
The Picture of Dorian
   Gray
Poems of W.B. Yeats:
   The Rose
Portrait of the Artist as a
   Young Man
Pride and Prejudice
Prometheus Bound

Pudd'nhead Wilson
Pygmalion
Rabbit, Run
A Raisin in the Sun
The Real Life of
   Sebastian Knight
Red Badge of Courage
The Republic
Richard II
Richard III
The Rime of the Ancient
   Mariner
Robinson Crusoe
Roll of Thunder, Hear
   My Cry
Romeo and Juliet
A Room of One's Own
A Room With a View
Rosencrantz and
   Guildenstern Are
   Dead
Salome
The Scarlet Letter
The Scarlet Pimpernel
Secret Sharer
Sense and Sensibility
A Separate Peace
Shakespeare's Sonnets
Siddhartha
Silas Marner
Sir Gawain and the
   Green Knight
Sister Carrie
Six Characters in Search
   of an Author
Slaughterhouse Five

Snow Falling on Cedars
The Social Contract
Something Wicked This
   Way Comes
Song of Roland
Song of Solomon
Sons and Lovers
The Sorrows of Young
   Werther
The Sound and the Fury
The Spanish Tragedy
Spring Awakening
The Stranger
A Streetcar Named
   Desire
The Sun Also Rises
Tale of Two Cities
The Taming of the Shrew
The Tempest
Tender is the Night
Tess of the D'Urbervilles
Their Eyes Were
   Watching God
Things Fall Apart
The Threepenny Opera
The Time Machine
Titus Andronicus
To Build a Fire
To Kill a Mockingbird
To the Lighthouse
Treasure Island
Troilus and Cressida
Turn of the Screw
Twelfth Night
Ulysses
Uncle Tom's Cabin

For our full list of over 250 Study Guides, Quizzes,
Sample College Application Essays, Literature Essays and E-texts, visit:

www.gradesaver.com

ClassicNotes

GrAdeSaver™

Getting you the grade since 1999™

Other ClassicNotes from GradeSaver™

Utopia
A Very Old Man With
   Enormous Wings
Villette
The Visit
Volpone
Waiting for Godot
Waiting for Lefty
Walden
Washington Square
The Waste Land
Where the Red Fern
   Grows
White Fang
White Noise
White Teeth
Who's Afraid of Virginia
   Woolf
Wide Sargasso Sea
Winesburg, Ohio
The Winter's Tale
Woyzeck
Wuthering Heights
The Yellow Wallpaper
Yonnondio: From the
   Thirties

For our full list of over 250 Study Guides, Quizzes,
Sample College Application Essays, Literature Essays and E-texts, visit:

www.gradesaver.com

Made in the USA
Lexington, KY
25 July 2014